WORKBOOK

FOR

12 RULES FOR LIFE

BY JORDAN B. PETERSON

An Antidote to Chaos

BY

BRIGHTEN BOOKS

CW01064852

COPYRIGHT

This publication is protected under the US Copyright Act of 1976 and other applicable international, federal, state, and local laws. All rights are reserved, including resale rights. You are not allowed to reproduce, transmit or sell this book in parts or in full without the written permission of the publisher. Printed in the USA. Copyright © 2020. Brighten Books.

DISCLAIMER

This book is a WORKBOOK. It is meant to be a companion, not a replacement, to the main book. Please note that this workbook is not authorized, licensed, approved, or endorsed by the author or publisher of the main book. The author of this workbook is wholly responsible for the content of this workbook and is not associated with the original author or publisher of the main book in any way. If you are looking to purchase a copy of the main book, please visit Amazon's website and search for **"12 Rules for Life: An Antidote to Chaos by Jordan B. Peterson"**.

INTRODUCTION: HOW TO USE THIS WORKBOOK

This is a companion workbook to the 12 RULES FOR LIFE by Jordan B. Peterson. This workbook has extracted the essential principles, lessons, guidelines and tips shared in the book and is now presenting them to you in an excellently creative format evoking real-life applications that will help you to learn, take action and effectively apply the lessons and guidelines from the book to your daily life.

You will benefit in the following ways from this workbook:

•   Lessons are presented to you in ways that are creative and tasking enough for the lessons to sink into your memory for your understanding and easy application in your daily life.

•   Each chapter's lessons are outlined for you under "Lessons" for easy identification and understanding. These the key points, the main point of the chapter that you need to note.

•   Instructive quizzes and knowledge tests are included under "Knowledge Check" to refresh your memory and consolidate your knowledge of the chapter's lessons. These are designed to get you to think profoundly about the lessons you have learned.

•   Action Items are included for you under "Action Steps". Probing, tasking, demanding, yet easy to complete if you mean business, these items are designed to engage you to become proactive and persistent and to begin to act, to take action on specific areas of your life, based on the several lessons and guidelines from the book.

•   A "Checklist" is included at the end of each chapter and this contains a list of the items you are encouraged to go through every day to consolidate your knowledge and support the transformative behavioral changes that would be happening in your life.

• A "Master Checklist" is included at the end of the workbook which brings together all the points that you must remember and all the action items that you must complete in order for the transformation to begin to happen in your life. You are to continue reviewing this Master Checklist everyday even after you have finished reading the workbook. This priceless Master Checklist will be your authentic guidepost to consolidating and sustaining the transformative change that you now own. Hold on to that list!

• Much lined-spaces are provided for you to jot down your answers to quizzes and exercises or for you to just doodle on about your thoughts at the end of each chapter.

• Do not leave any exercises undone. You do not have to do all at the same time, but ensure that you complete all the exercises. They are all for your own good. And they are all FUN!

This book is a companion WORKBOOK. The goal of this WORKBOOK is to nudge you and help you to become proactive, to take action and to begin to apply the lessons and principles from the book (12 RULES FOR LIFE by Jordan Peterson) to your daily life. Remember that it takes enough intellectual provocation, emotional instigation and daily practice, repetition and perseverance to create transformative change in your life. This WORKBOOK will get you there!

TABLE OF CONTENTS

RULE 1: STAND UP STRAIGHT WITH YOUR SHOULDERS BACK

LESSONS

1. The dominance hierarchy (a.k.a social status, social hierarchy, the pecking order, etc.) has persisted and impacted life on earth for approximately 500 million years. Humans and the other species have long lived in the dominance hierarchy and have been struggling for status and position right from the beginning of everything. The dominance hierarchy is as ancient as the conglomeration of the first set of cells from which every life form eventually evolved. Indeed, the dominance hierarchy has become permanent, real and natural.

2. There is an extremely ancient and basic part of the human brain that monitors our position in the dominance hierarchy. This part or zone in the brain is in fact a dominance calculator (and serotonin dealer). This dominance calculator monitors exactly where you are positioned in the dominance hierarchy in your society, or your territory. It perennially observes how you are treated by other people. It assesses your position; determines your value; and then assigns you a status on the dominance hierarchy. And on the basis of that assigned position, it either increases or restricts serotonin availability to you.

3. Serotonin is a chemical and a neurotransmitter found in the human body. It supposedly regulates social behavior and mood. It also regulates sleep, appetite, sexual desire, sexual function, memory, and digestion. Serotonin also contributes to happiness and wellbeing. Scientific research evidence supports the association of low levels of serotonin with depression.

4. The top of the dominance hierarchy is a favored place to be. If you belong here, you have a high social status. You are safe, secure, productive and well connected to the right social networks. As a consequence of belonging to this class, the dominance calculator in your brain will deal you an increased availability and flow of serotonin which will make you calmer, more relaxed, and cause you to stand up straight, with your shoulders back, and become ever more confident, stable, reliable, productive, successful and fulfilled.

5. The bottom of the dominance hierarchy, on the other hand, is a bad, sad and dangerous place to belong. If you belong here, you are of low status and you are beset with all manner of problems, issues and negative life circumstances. And so the dominance calculator in your brain decreases the availability of serotonin to you and

causes you to become hyper-cautious, hype alert, overly reactive (both physically and psychologically), impulsive and likely to live and die carelessly. Alas! If only you could get just a little more of that darned serotonin!

6. It is very important to note that the dominance calculator can, sometimes, malfunction. To prevent this, embrace routine and predictability in your daily activities. Automatize your daily activities.

7. Wake up from sleep in the morning at approximately the same time regardless of what time you went to bed the night before.

8. Ensure that your breakfast contains fat and is protein-laden, and that you eat breakfast as soon as you wake up.

9. Also beware of being trapped in a positive feedback loop which can intensify and amplify your reality to a point where it becomes distorted and out of control.

10. And be aware that several systems of interaction between the brain, the body and the social world can get trapped into positive feedback loops, all of which can disrupt the dominance calculator in your brain.

11. Furthermore, be aware that the dominance calculator can transform a traumatic experience that you may have gone through to the extent that it makes it more likely (not less likely) that you will experience similar traumatic events again.

12. Note that the dominance calculator can, in fact, be disrupted. You must be aware of this, and you may wish to guard against it.

13. And, be like the WINNER-LOBSTER. By this I mean, fix your posture. Stand straight. Straighten your back. and pull back your shoulders. Strut about your territory, cockily, a little. Demand more respect and fair treatment from others. Live like royalty and live with aplomb. This will improve how you view yourself and how you feel about yourself. And it will improve how others view and treat you, kicking off a virtuous cycle.

14. Do not be like the LOSER-LOBSTER. Do not habitually slouch, sulk, avoid eye contact, disappear at the first sign of conflict, or engage in other mannerisms or allow other appearances that convey defeat, subordination and low status to others. Beware that this may set you off into a positive feedback loop situation.

15. Finally, and very importantly remember that your dominance calculator is always right there in your brain, ever present, watching closely and carefully, recording everything, calculating and judging your value. And remember that it will eventually assign you your position on the dominance hierarchy. And if you did okay, you may just get an ampler supply of serotonin. But if you did badly, not only will your supply

of serotonin get decreased (perhaps drastically), but you also may just get to spend more time in the Hobbesian bottom world hell.

KNOWLEDGE CHECK

1. Under Rule 1, Peterson writes that throughout nature, abilities within and among the species are not equal; that abilities vary naturally, but that those with stronger or more abilities control more of the available resources.
(i) Do you agree? Explain.
(ii) Identify and discuss one current ideology that disagrees with this position.

_____

_____

_____

_____

2. Under Rule 1, Peterson also discusses the "dominance hierarchy" and the "dominance calculator".
(i) Explain the dominance hierarchy and the dominance calculator. What is the difference between these two concepts?
(ii) Are both concepts natural? Explain how both may have become natural?

_____

_____

_____

_____

3. Under Rule 1, Peterson also discusses "order" and "chaos". Discuss both concepts and specifically explain the relationship between the two.

_____

_____

_____

_____

4. What is serotonin? Describe its role, functions and effects. Explain the connection between one's position on the dominance hierarchy and the availability of serotonin in the one's body.

_____

_____

_____

_____

5. Under Rule 1, Peterson also discusses the concept of the "positive feedback loop". Explain the concept of the "positive feedback loop".

_____

_____

_____

_____

6. Under Rule 1, Peterson explains that territory does not matter; that there is no primal urge in all creatures to dominate a territory; that co-habitation within a specific territory very rarely breeds conflict; and that it is only lobsters that fight for territory. Is this true or false? (Check one):
True   [   ]
False   [   ]

7.   Under Rule 1, Peterson also explains that individuals who belong in the bottom of the dominance hierarchy are of low status and are beset with all manner of problems and negative life circumstances. They are hyper-cautious, hype alert, overly reactive, impulsive and likely to live and die carelessly. Is this true or false? (Check one):
True   [   ]
False   [   ]

8. The dominance calculator decreases the availability of serotonin to those individuals who belong in the bottom of the dominance hierarchy. Is this true or false? (Check one):
True   [   ]
False   [   ]

9. Peterson prescribes that in order to prevent your dominance calculator from malfunction you have to embrace routine and predictability in your daily activities. You have to automatize your daily activities. Is this true or false? (Check one):

True   [   ]
False   [   ]

10. According to Peterson, a defeated human acts in much the same way as a defeated dog or a defeated lobster, in that they all display the physical signs of defeat, surrender and subordination, primarily through posture and other behavioral signs. Is this true or false? (Check one):

True   [   ]
False   [   ]

ACTION STEPS

1. What do you consider to be your territory? Describe your position within the dominance hierarchy in your territory and explain how you got to that position.

_____

_____

_____

_____

2. Assuming that you are unsatisfied with your position on the dominance hierarchy in your territory, articulate a step-by-step plan of how you would go about renegotiating your position on that dominance hierarchy within the next six months.

_____

_____

_____

_____

3. Negotiating or maintaining a position on the dominance hierarchy can be fraught with great difficulties. It can be prosecuted via phased confrontation. But physical prowess is not the only way. Forming and using a supportive, all-inclusive network of loyal allies is also another way. Explain what you understand by this strategy and articulate a plan of how you will go about forming and sustaining your very own "supportive, all-inclusive network of loyal allies" in your territory.

_____

_____

_____

_____

4. Under Rule I, Peterson prescribes that sleep should be automatized, particularly wakeup times; that wakeup times should be in the morning at approximately the same time regardless of what time one went to bed the night before. Explain why this is important and articulate a detailed plan of how you will automatize your wakeup time.

_____

_____

_____

_____

5. Under Rule I, Peterson also prescribes that breakfast ought to contain fat and protein and should be eaten as soon as one wakes up. Explain why this is important and articulate a detailed plan of how you will henceforth incorporate healthy natural fats and protein in your breakfast and how you will ensure that you eat breakfast early.

_____

_____

_____

_____

6. Itemize any positive feedback loops that are currently in your life and articulate a detailed plan of how you will address and resolve each one of them.

_____

_____

_____

_____

7. Under Rule 1, Peterson advises that you should carry yourself like the WINNER-LOBSTER.
(i) What does he mean by this?
(ii) Why is this important?
(iii) How would you act and carry yourself like the WINNER LOBSTER?

_____

_____

_____

_____

8. Conversely, Peterson also advises against acting or carrying yourself like the LOSER-LOBSTER.
(i) What does he mean by this?
(ii) Why is this important?
(iii) How would you act and carry yourself like a LOSER LOBSTER?

_____

_____

_____

_____

_____

_____

[   ] I acknowledge that territory matters and that social status matters too. In fact, as much as territory matters, social status also, almost equally matters. Both are extremely vital for survival.

[   ] I shall take daily steps (even if micro steps) to establish or maintain enough dominance within my territory to enable me to survive and to live in social harmony with other co-inhabitants in my territory.

[   ] I acknowledge that throughout nature, abilities within and among the species are not equal. And that those with stronger or more abilities control more of the available resources. Thus, I shall take daily steps to develop myself and increase my abilities.

[   ] I acknowledge that negotiating or maintaining a social status (a position within the dominance hierarchy in any given territory) is characteristically fraught with great difficulties (which are more or less inevitable). I am not intimidated by those difficulties.

[   ] I acknowledge that phased confrontation is one way to renegotiate or maintain one's position on the dominance hierarchy. But it is not the only way. Other attributes are important including forming beneficial alliances with loyal subordinates and paying attention to and cooperating with the females and the young. I shall come up with a step-by-step plan and take daily steps towards forming beneficial alliances within my territory, paying attention to and cooperating with the females and the young within my territory.

[   ] I acknowledge that the dominance hierarchy or negotiating a good position within it is not Machiavellian or evil. This is because the dominance hierarchy is natural. It has existed for a long time (approximately 500 million years). And it has been selected by nature for eons. It has impacted life on earth for eons thus it is "natural", ancient, real and permanent.

[   ] I acknowledge the importance of serotonin. It governs posture and it impacts positioning within the dominance hierarchy. And higher levels (not lower levels) of serotonin are more desirable.

[   ] I shall boost my serotonin levels via eating a healthy, pro-serotonin diet, exercising regularly, getting enough sunshine or light therapy, getting a massage from time to time, avoiding stress, maintaining a positive outlook and maintaining a healthy microbiome.

[   ] I acknowledge that the dominance calculator can be disrupted or distorted. Thus I shall avoid all negative habits that can lead to that end including (i) positive feedback

loops, (ii) addiction to alcohol or drugs (iii) anxiety disorder - e.g. agoraphobia, (iv) depression, (v) and isolation, etc.

[ ] I also acknowledge that the dominance calculator can sometimes, malfunction. To prevent this, I shall take steps to incorporate predictability and routine in my daily activities. I shall make effort to automatize my daily activities.

[ ] I shall wake up from sleep every morning early (no later than 6AM) regardless of what time I went to bed the night before.

[ ] I shall ensure that my breakfast contains enough protein and healthy fats and that I eat breakfast early (as soon as you wake up).

[ ] I shall henceforth be and act like the WINNER-LOBSTER. I shall henceforth fix my posture, stand up straight, pull my shoulders back and walk with confidence. I shall demand more respect and fair treatment from others. I shall henceforth live with panache and aplomb.

[ ] I shall henceforth no more act like a LOSER-LOBSTER. Never again shall I slouch, sulk, avoid eye contact, disappear at the first sign of conflict, or engage in any other mannerisms or allow any other appearances that convey defeat, subordination and low status to others!

[ ] I am a winner because I said so. I am the WINNER-LOBSTER because I said so. And I shall henceforth live every day of my life as the winner that I am. I am worthy of respect, belonging, loving and being loved. And I am enough in every respect (despite whatever imperfections and vulnerabilities that I may have). My imperfections and vulnerabilities are irrelevant. I am still a winner because I said so. I am still the WINNER-LOBSTER because I said so.

RULE 2: TREAT YOURSELF LIKE SOMEONE YOU ARE RESPONSIBLE FOR HELPING

LESSONS

1. Chaos is fundamentally formless potential. It is an unexplored, uncharted territory of limitless possibilities. Chaos is a dominion of unstructured, unformed, unsorted, un-schemed, and un-harmonized force and potential, replete with infinite permutations and possibilities. In fact, it is an "un-dominion", as a dominion itself implies some type of structure, some understood expression. Chaos is the obverse. Chaos is the unknown. It is from chaos (this formless potential), that God in the "Priestly" account of Creation called up order in Creation, and called forth (created) man in His Own Image, using His spoken Word.

2. Order, on the other hand, is a form, a structure, the domain of known, understood, and expected things. It is territory already explored and charted. Order is certainty and uniformity, purity, predictability, stability, clarity and light. In order's realm, things are and act as God intended them to, that is, order is harmonious, un-chaotic, structured, stable, predictable, known and understood.

3. Perception of meaning of things or of things as personalities or entities occurs before or in concert with perception of things as objects. We see what things mean, their purpose and intent, just as fast as or faster than we see what they are as objects (via the operation of the so-called "hyperactive agency detector" that is innate in us).

4. Man's most fundamental category through which he interprets everything is that of the "structured, creative opposition", that is, male and female. This division or categorization is so primordial, and so much a part of man's evolutionary environment that it has become internalized and embedded deep within man's psyche, being.

5. Order appears to be categorized as male. Order is the head, the ruler, the rule maker, the rules, and the enforcer of rules. Order is the guardian, the rewarder and the punisher. It is the culture, the environment, the system. Order is the known, the familiar, the predictable.

6. Chaos appears to be categorized as female, the eternal feminine. This is because chaos is the unknown and what we have come to know emanated from the unknown, that is,

from chaos, just as all beings came from mothers. Thus chaos is the source, the begetter, birthplace, the formative material of all things

7. Man exists in order, the known and the predictable, which is at the same time encircled by chaos, the unknown and the unpredictable. But to straddle both worlds is to be balanced. It is the proper place to be. It is the place that man ought to be. This is where man finds meaning.

8. Self-loathing (emanating from the sin and fall of man, a capacity for malevolence that is quite unique in the world of living things) is the simple reason why some people will take care to buy and carefully administer prescription medication on their pet, but would not do the same for themselves. Why would anyone care for anything as naked, ugly, wicked, disloyal, disobedient, worthless, cowardly and dishonorable as man (or as himself/ herself).

9. Some people take the idea of virtuous self-sacrifice too far, sacrificing and victimizing themselves for the interest of others. This is wrong. To do so is to support tyranny. There is no virtue in allowing oneself to be victimized and turned into a slave.

10. You have an obligation to others outside of yourself to take good care of yourself. There is a spark of God in you which does not belong to you, but to God alone. So take care of yourself. You are not just yours alone to subject to any kind of maltreatment. Instead, love yourself and treat yourself with respect, kindness, and care.

11. Always consider the future and think of what your life would look of tomorrow if you took good care of yourself today. Think of career, health, family, finances, the spiritual etc. Articulate, by yourself, your own principles, so that way you can guard against being taken advantage of.

12. Discipline yourself properly. Keep promises, especially those you make to yourself. Reward yourself. It motivates you and builds your trust in yourself.

13. Be careful how you act towards yourself, and ensure that you act towards yourself only in ways that are likely to guide you towards becoming a good person.

14. Hang on to your vision and direction. Never lose them for they are unstoppable forces that will turn the obstacles in your way into victories and opportunities.

15. Look after yourself. Define your own identity. Carve your own niche. Improve your personality. Make your life choices carefully and articulate your Being.

16. Devote your life to making the world a better place. That will cure you of a miserable existence. It will give strong meaning to your life. It will cushion you from the privations and suffering required by Being. And it will bring you closer to walking with God.

17. Strengthen the individual starting with yourself. Treat yourself with respect, kindness, and care.

KNOWLEDGE CHECK

1. Under Rule 2, Peterson laments that many people care for their pets more than they care for themselves; that they are better at ensuring that their pets' medications are correctly administered on the pets than they are at taking their own medications.
(i) How does Peterson eventually explain this phenomenon?
(ii) Do you agree or disagree with him? Explain.

_____

_____

_____

_____

2. Under Rule 2, Peterson discusses the two different stories of Creation from two different Middle Eastern sources. Name and describe the first of these two stories. Be sure to explain what the creative force (the fundamental ingredient of creation) was, under the first story of Creation.

_____

_____

_____

_____

3. Name and describe the second of the two stories of Creation. And explain the connection between this second story of Creation and the observation that some people ensure to buy and carefully administer prescription medication on their pets, but would not do the same for themselves?

_____

_____

_____

_____

4. Is continued self-loathing (emanating from the original sin and fall of man) still justified? Articulate your understanding of Peterson's answer to this question.

_____

_____

_____

_____

5. Under Rule 2, Peterson states that to truly understand the first story of creation, it would be necessary to first understand the primordial world, the pre-science, ancient, worldview and assumptions from whence that first story of Creation sprung. Describe this primordial world and its assumptions.

_____

_____

_____

_____

6. Scientific truths emerged only just about 500 years ago. Is this true or false? (Check one):
True   [   ]
False   [   ]

7. Under the pre-science, ancient, worldview, that gave birth to the first story of Creation, Being was understood as residing in action, reminiscent of an unfolding drama or story, a lived experience, subjective in manifestation and significance, difficult if not impossible to reduce to a detached, objective expression as would be the case in a scientific description. Is this true or false? (Check one):
True   [   ]
False   [   ]

8. The fundamental constituents of the primordial world of experience from which the first story of Creation came are: (i) chaos, (ii) order, (iii) and process (that is, the process via which both chaos and order interface). Is this true or false? (Check one):
True   [   ]
False   [   ]

9. According to Peterson, human beings exist in order but are simultaneously encircled by chaos. It is, however, when man mediates between this duality, when man treads the border between these worlds that man can engage meaningfully. Is this true or false? (Check one):

True   [   ]
False   [   ]

10. Man finds meaning when ensconced in chaos (not when ensconced in order or when straddled between both worlds. Is this true or false? (Check one):

True   [   ]
False   [   ]

11. Under Rule 2, Peterson discusses a primordial world of experience (the world of the "Priestly" account of Creation) and the more recent scientific world. Based on Peterson's exposition of these two worlds, compare and contrast the two worlds, in detail.

_____

_____

_____

_____

12. Under Rule 2, Peterson discusses "chaos".
(i) Describe chaos as he explained it.
(ii) What is the connection between chaos and the first story of Creation?
(iii) Why is chaos categorized as female?

_____

_____

_____

_____

13. Under Rule 2, Peterson also discusses "order".
(i) Describe order as he explained it.
(ii) Explain why order is categorized as male?
(iii) Peterson also describes order as being destructive when overstretched or taken to extremes. Explain.

_____

_____

_____

_____

14. "Self-loathing emanating from the original sin and the fall of man (recounted in the Jawhist account of creation)" is the answer to what question?

_____

_____

_____

_____

15. *Peterson's message in Rule 2 appears to be as follows: "That since the original sin and the fall of man, humans have been trying to see the face of God again, trying to get back to walking with God, again. In doing so, some now practice virtuous self-sacrifice. But some have taken the idea of virtuous self-sacrifice too far, allowing themselves to suffer, be abused, victimized and turned into slaves in the service of others. This is wrong for the following reasons:*

(1) It is wrong because it is to support tyranny.
(2) It is also wrong because a human being does not solely belong to him/herself alone. There are others (like family and friends) who share in the fate of the human being. So you have an obligation to other people outside of yourself to take good care of yourself. Therefore, you must never abuse yourself or allow yourself to be abused. In that sense, then, you should not fail to take your medication or fail to take care of yourself.
(3) It is also wrong because there is a part of the human being (indeed, the whole) that belongs to God which we must take care of. We, therefore, must never abuse that vessel which belongs to God or allow it to be abused by others. So, in this sense, again, you should not fail to take your medication or fail to care for yourself.

So what is the proper way forward? The proper way forward is to treat yourself as if you were someone you are responsible for helping. Love yourself and treat yourself with respect, kindness, and care. In that sense, then, take your medications. Take care of yourself. Love yourself. To fail to do so is to support tyranny, to be irresponsible to others who share you with you, to be disrespectful of God's vessel and thus to fall further away from God, even after your original sin and the fall of man.

Write a 1000-word essay in support or in opposition to this message.

16. Now, based on all the above, why should you ensure that you fill your prescriptions and take your medication properly?

_____

_____

_____

_____

ACTION STEPS

1. Peterson advises that you should always consider the future and think of what your life would look like tomorrow, if you took good care of yourself today. Write down a step-by-step plan of how you intend to, henceforth, take good care of your **career** today so as to ensure a better tomorrow.

_____

_____

_____

_____

2. Write down a step-by-step plan of how you intend to, henceforth, take good care of your **health** today so as to ensure a healthier tomorrow.

_____

_____

_____

_____

3. Write down a step-by-step plan of how you intend to, henceforth, take good care of your **family** today so as to ensure a better tomorrow.

_____

_____

_____

_____

4. Write down a step-by-step plan of how you intend to, henceforth, take good care of your *finances* today so as to ensure a better tomorrow.

_____

_____

_____

_____

5. Write down a step-by-step plan of how you intend to, henceforth, take good care of your **spirituality** today so as to ensure a peaceful tomorrow.

_____

_____

_____

_____

6. Write down a step-by-step plan of how you intend to, henceforth, take good care of your **social networks** today so as to ensure a healthy socially connected tomorrow.

_____

_____

_____

_____

7. Peterson also advises that you should discipline yourself properly. Do you have a self-discipline plan? How would you discipline yourself? Write down a step-by-step plan of how you intend to, henceforth, grow and develop your **self-discipline.**

_____

_____

8. Peterson also advises that you should **keep promises, especially those you make to yourself.** Write down two lists: (i) a list of promises that you made to people in the past 12 months that you fulfilled (ii) and a list of promises that you made to people in the past 12 months that you did not fulfill. Write down a step-by-step of how you intend to recompense for those promises you broke.

_____

_____

_____

_____

8. Also write down another two lists: (i) a list of promises that you made to yourself people in the past 12 months that you fulfilled (ii) and a list of promises that you made to yourself in the past 12 months that you did not fulfill. Write down a step-by-step of how you intend to recompense for those promises to yourself that you broke.

_____

_____

_____

_____

9. Do you **reward yourself** for your accomplishments great and small? Write down two lists: (i) minor accomplishments for which you rewarded yourself and what type of reward (ii) and significant accomplishments for which you rewarded yourself and what type of reward. If you do not reward yourself, then write down a step-by-step plan of how you intend to incorporate self-reward into your personal development program.

_____

_____

_____

_____

10. Peterson also advises that you should be careful **how you act towards yourself**, and ensure that you act towards yourself only in ways that are likely to guide you towards becoming a good person. Write down two lists: (i) a list of your positive acts towards yourself that will help you to become a good person (ii) and a list of your negative acts towards yourself that are likely to militate against you becoming a good person. Then write down a step-by-step plan of how you intend to address those negative acts towards yourself that are keeping you from becoming a good person.

_____

_____

_____

_____

11. Write down **your vision and direction in life** and your step-by-step plan of how you intend to realize them.

_____

_____

_____

_____

12. Write down your step-by-step plan of how you intend to realize **define your own identity, articulate your own Being and carve your own niche**.

_____

_____

_____

_____

13. Write down your step-by-step plan of how you intend to **improve your personality**.

_____

_____

14. Write down your step-by-step plan of how you intend to **make the world a better place**.

_____

_____

_____

_____

15. How do you plan to **bring yourself closer to God and maintain a close relationship with God**?

_____

_____

_____

_____

CHECKLIST

[   ] I shall not indulge in self-loathing (despite man's original sin and the subsequent fall of man. I am not naked, ugly, wicked, disloyal, disobedient, worthless, cowardly or dishonorable. I have been redeemed by the grace of God.

[   ] I acknowledge that the way forward now is to work on improving myself to earn my place besides God, again. In all my thoughts, words and deeds I shall strive for virtue and the good.

[   ] I acknowledge that virtuous self-sacrifice is good. But I shall not take it too far. I shall not allow myself to be victimized, or abused or to be turned into a slave for the interest of others. There is no virtue in that.

[   ] I acknowledge that I have an obligation to my family, friends and others outside of yourself to take good care of myself and I shall henceforth never cease to take good care of myself, love myself and treat myself with respect and kindness, always.

[ ] I acknowledge that there is a spark of God in me which does not belong to me, but to God alone, thus that I am a vessel that contains a quantity of God. I, therefore, acknowledge that it is my obligation to take good care of me (God's vessel) and I shall henceforth never cease to take good care of myself, love myself and treat myself with respect and kindness, always.

[ ] I shall not subject myself or allow anyone to subject me to any kind of maltreatment or abuse.

[ ] If I see any signs or symptoms of ill health in me, I shall seek medical intervention immediately. If I am prescribed medication, I shall fill my prescriptions and take my medication faithfully, as directed.

[ ] I shall always consider the future and make good plans for my career, health, family, finances, spirituality etc.; and work my plans, diligently, for a prosperous future.

[ ] I shall articulate, by myself, my own vision and principles in life and define my own identity, so as to have a clear direction in my life and so as to guard against being taken advantage of. And I shall hang on to my vision, principles and direction in life for a purposeful and fulfilling life.

[ ] I shall make my life choices very carefully in order to articulate my Being.

[ ] I shall not allow myself to succumb to indiscipline. Instead I shall pursue a course of self-discipline.

[ ] I shall keep all my promises, especially those that I make to myself.

[ ] I shall always reward myself for my accomplishments (great or small) so as to motivate myself and build trust with myself.

[ ] I shall exercise great care in how I act towards myself, and I shall ensure that I act towards myself only in ways that are likely to guide me towards becoming a good person.

[ ] I shall invest in my personal growth and in improving my personality

[ ] I shall devote my life to making the world a better place and I shall start by strengthening the individual, starting with myself.

[ ] I shall strive always to bring myself closer to God.

RULE 3: MAKE FRIENDS WITH PEOPLE WHO WANT THE BEST FOR YOU

LESSONS

1. Choose friendships that will improve your life. Never have a low opinion of yourself. Always know that you deserve better and that you are responsible for creating your own world by yourself with the tools you have at hand.

2. Be wary of associating with losers or attempting to rescue a habitual loser. Not every loser is a victim; and not every loser wishes to be rescued or saved.

3. Note that your desire to rescue a loser could be motivated by (i) your narcissism and vanity; (ii) or your desire to draw attention to your infinite reserves of compassion and good-will; (iii) or your desire to appear virtuous; (iv) or your desire to display an independent strength of character.

4. You have no moral obligation to make friends with, or to support, or to rescue a habitual loser. In fact, beware of making friends with such individuals. They are likely to discourage you, lower your standards, and become jealous of your success, and eventually drag you down.

5. Beware of overly uncritical, overly pitiful, overly compassionate so-called "loser/ friends". They are ushers into the "hallowed" halls of mediocrity and worse yet, failure.

6. Be warned that it is possible that you may come to ruin as a consequence of your attempt to pull up an un-repentant, habitual loser. Losing can be infectious, and going down is easier than climbing up.

7. Instead, make friends with good, healthy people. And there is nothing wrong in doing so. Good healthy friends will provide you with constructive criticism, provide you with worthy examples, raise your standards, save you from destructive behavior, and you can mutually improve each other's lives. Iron sharpens iron.

8. Before you help someone, find out the cause of the person's problems. Do not assume that they are an innocent victim of unjust life circumstances. It is never that simple. If you absolve the person completely of any personal responsibility for their life circumstances, you invariably deny the person of all past, present, and future agency.

Thus you relieve him or her of all power. Help only those that want to be helped, and that can be helped.

9. Here is a rule you may adopt regarding making friends: if you cannot recommend any friend of yours to become friends with your son, father, or sister, then why would you still keep such a friend for yourself?

KNOWLEDGE CHECK

1. According to Peterson, another one of the reasons why people choose friends, places and situations that are not good for them could be because of **their own limitations, nascent illnesses and past traumas.** Is this true or false? (Check one):
True   [   ]
False   [   ]

2. According to Peterson, another one of the reasons why people choose friends, places and situations that are not good for them could be because **they have a low opinion of their own worth**, **believing that they do not deserve any better.** Is this true or false? (Check one):
True   [   ]
False   [   ]

3. According to Peterson, another one of the reasons why people choose friends, places and situations that are not good for them could be because **they do not want the "trouble" that comes with "better" (more like a Freudian drive to repeat past mistakes).** Is this true or false? (Check one):
True   [   ]
False   [   ]

4. According to Peterson, another one of the reasons why people choose friends, places and situations that are not good for them could be because **they have a desire to rescue someone**. Is this true or false? (Check one):
True   [   ]
False   [   ]

5. According to Peterson, another one of the reasons why people choose friends, places and situations that are not good for them could be **just because it's easier**. Is this true or false? (Check one):
True   [   ]
False   [   ]

6. Under Rule 3, Peterson delineates four motivations that could possibly compel people to choose friends that are not good for them just because they have the desire to rescue someone.

30

(i) What are these four motivations? Itemize and describe them.
(ii) Discuss and critique these four motivations.

_____

_____

_____

_____

7. Under Rule 3, Petersons states as follows: "***you have no moral obligation to support someone who is making the world a worse place. Instead you should choose people who want things to be better, not worse***". Do you agree or disagree with this statement? Explain your position in detail.

_____

_____

_____

_____

8. Under Rule 3, Peterson provides some guidelines to follow in deciding whether or not to help someone. He also prescribes a rule of thumb to follow in deciding whether or not to make someone your friend.
(i) Itemize and discuss those guidelines and advice that Peterson prescribed for deciding whether or not to help someone.
(ii) Critique the rule of thumb that Peterson prescribed for deciding whether or not to make someone your friend.

_____

_____

_____

_____

9. Under Rule 3, Peterson discusses the so-called "trouble" and "unease" that comes with choosing and having those "better" friends that are actually better for us. He, nevertheless, prescribes that we should surround ourselves with good healthy, wholesome friends.

(i) Articulate your understanding of what Peterson means by the "trouble" and "unease" that comes with choosing and having those "better" friends that are actually better for us. (ii) Discuss Peterson's reasoning that we should, nevertheless, surround ourselves with good healthy, wholesome friends.

_____

_____

_____

_____

10. So, why are some people unable or unwilling to move or to change their friendships and improve their lives? Why do such people continually choose friends who are not good for them, and live in places and tolerate situations and conditions that are not good for them?
(i) Write a 1000-word answer to this question based on Peterson's arguments in answer to this question.

_____

_____

_____

_____

_____

_____

_____

_____

_____

_____

ACTION STEPS

1. Peterson advises that you should never have a low opinion of yourself and that you should always know that you deserve better.
(i) Does your life currently reflect the above values? Think about that.
(ii) Then, write out a list of ten significant things that you will accomplish in the next six months that will serve as evidence that you do not have a low opinion of yourself and that you know that you deserve better.

_____

_____

_____

_____

2. Peterson advises that you should choose your friends carefully and that you should choose friendships that will improve your life.
(i) Compile a list of your current friends and for each friend write whether and how they are improving your life (List A).
(ii) Compile a list of those who are not currently your friends, but who you wish to make friends because you know they will improve your life (List B).
(iii) Then write out a step-by-step plan of how you wish to initiate friendship with those on List B.

_____

_____

_____

_____

3. Peterson also advises that you are responsible for creating your own world by yourself with the tools you have at hand.
(i) Write down the type of world you want for yourself and express it as 12 major goals you want to achieve in your life.
(ii) Compile an exhaustive list of the tools you have at hand with which to achieve those goals.
(iii) Then write out a step-by-step plan of how you intend to achieve those 12 major goals with the tools you have at hand.

_____

_____

_____

_____

4. Peterson warns that you should be wary of associating with losers or attempting to rescue a habitual loser.

(i) Compile a list of those that you are currently associating with who you consider to be losers. And for each name indicate why you consider the person a loser.

(ii) For each name on the above list, write down your justification for continuing to associate with that person despite that you consider the person to be a loser.

_____

_____

_____

_____

5. For each "loser" in the list you compiled in item 4 above, consider what your motivation may be for associating with/rescuing that "loser" against the backdrop of the check list provided by Peterson to wit: that you may be motivated by (i) your narcissism and vanity; (ii) or your desire to draw attention to your infinite reserves of compassion and good-will; (iii) or your desire to appear virtuous; (iv) or your desire to display an independent strength of character. Then write down your observations.

_____

_____

_____

_____

6. Peterson also warns that _you have no moral obligation to make friends with, or to support, or to rescue a habitual loser._ In fact, he admonishes against making friends with such individuals. Do you understand why you should not make friends with losers? Describe all the reasons for not doing such that Peterson articulated under Rule 3 and add other reasons of your own.

_____

_____

_____

_____

_____

_____

_____

7. Peterson strongly suggests that *you should, instead, make friends with good, healthy people and that there is nothing wrong in doing so*. Do you understand why you should *make friends with good, healthy people, why such is good for you?* Describe all the reasons for doing so that Peterson articulated under Rule 3 and add other reasons of your own.

_____

_____

_____

_____

8. Peterson also warns that you should beware of those friends of yours who are too uncritical and too tolerant of everything you do and too pitiful of you because such friends do not challenge you enough and are simply guiding you down the path of mediocrity or failure.
(i) Compile a list of such friends in your life and articulate why you consider each person on that list an "unchallenging friend".
(ii) Then think carefully and articulate what you intend to do about each person on that list.

_____

_____

_____

_____

_____

9. What does Peterson suggest you do before you decide to help someone?

_____

_____

_____

_____

_____

10. Compile two lists of your friends: (i) first, a list of those friends of yours who you would not hesitate to recommend to become friends with your son, father, or sister (ii) and a list of those friends of yours who you would NEVER recommend to become friends with your son, father, or sister. (iii) Write a 1000-word statement of what you understand these two lists to mean, backed by Peterson's arguments under Rule 3 and other arguments of your own.

_____

_____

_____

_____

_____

_____

_____

_____

_____

_____

[   ] I shall make only those friendships that will improve your life. I shall review my life, henceforth, and continue only with those friendships that improve my life.

[   ] I shall never have a low opinion of yourself. I understand and acknowledge that I deserve better. Indeed, I deserve the best.

[   ] I acknowledge that I am responsible for creating my own world by myself with the tools I have at hand I shall create and maintain my best world for myself.

[   ] I shall avoid associating with losers.

[   ] I shall avoid attempting to rescue a habitual loser, noting that not every loser is a victim and not every loser wishes to be rescued or saved.

[   ] I acknowledge that I have no moral obligation to make friends with, or to support, or to rescue a habitual loser.

[   ] I understand that if I make friends with a loser, the loser will, eventually discourage me, lower my standards, become jealous of my accomplishments, and, eventually, drag me down.

[   ] I also understand that it is possible that I can come to ruin as a consequence of my attempt to pull up an un-repentant, habitual loser. I understand that being friends with a loser can infect me with losing, as losing can be infectious and going down is easier than climbing up.

[   ] I understand that overly uncritical, overly pitiful and overly compassionate "friends" are not good for me. Their lack of criticism, too much pity and too much compassion towards me will only, gradually, lead me to mediocrity and failure.

[   ] I shall, instead, make friends with good, healthy people who will provide me with constructive criticism, worthy examples, raise my standards and save me from destructive behavior. We can mutually improve each other's lives. Iron sharpens iron.

[   ] I shall, henceforth, before I decide to help someone, first find out the cause of the person's problems. I shall not automatically assume that the person is an innocent victim of unjust life circumstances. I shall help only those that want to be helped and that can be helped.

[   ] I hereby adopt this rule of thumb: ***if I would never recommend a person to become friends with my son, father, or sister, then I should never make such a person my friend or keep such a person as my friend***.

RULE 4: COMPARE YOURSELF TO WHO YOU WERE YESTERDAY, NOT TO WHO SOMEONE ELSE IS TODAY

LESSONS

1. The game you are playing is somehow rigged. So stop listening to that critical voice within you. Things are not always black-and-white, as your internal critic usually suggests. There are vital degrees and gradations of value which such a binary system (of black or white; good or bad) does not recognize, and the consequences are not good.

2. There is not just one game at which to succeed or fail. There are many games. If you don't succeed at one, you can try another. In other words, change the game. Pick something better matched to your unique mix of strengths, weaknesses and situation. Or, you can even invent a new game, a game that works for you.

3. Like most people you are most likely involved in many games (career, friends, family, personal projects, and miscellaneous pursuits). You will most likely perform to varying degrees of success or failure across all these games. But that is how it should be. Do not expect to win at everything! Note that growing might be the most important form of winning.

4. Do not compare yourself to others. The specifics of the many games you are playing are so unique to you, so comparison to others is simply inappropriate. You win some. You lose some. And you may be "so, so" at some. In any event, be grateful for what you have. Gratitude protects you against the feelings of victimhood and resentment.

5. Be more audacious. Be truthful. Engage and articulate yourself frankly. Manifest your dark and unspoken desires. Stop being afraid and stop pretending to be moral. Stop putting up with things, or pretending to like things just because of duty or obligation or because you wish to avoid conflict.

6. You are unique and individual. You are you, with your own specific problems, talents, wants, needs, values etc. These are what define your existence. Therefore, you must decide how much of your time to spend on the different sectors (games) of your life.

7. Find out who you are. Take stock of your flaws, faults, imperfections, inadequacies. Thereafter begin to address your faults. Address one adequacy in your life at a time.

Promise yourself a reward if you take some small steps towards your desired change. Go small. Do not go beyond the small steps that you have identified. Indeed, small steps and the promise of a reward are the secret. Continue doing this daily for three years and you would have transformed your life!

8.   People only see what they want to see. This is because sight depends on aim, and aim is a product of value. You see what you aim at, and you aim at only those things that you value. Thus you are indeed blinded to the rest of the world by your desires. This could be to your disadvantage when you are facing a crisis. To effect a transformative change, you need to let go of your idiosyncratic world view, your current knowledge, so that a new world of new possibilities will show itself to you.

9.   Pay attention and focus on your physical and psychological environment. And fix those things within that environment that bother you. To find such things, ask yourself three questions: (i) What is it that is troubling me?"; (ii) "Is it something that I am able to correct?"; (iii) "Am I actually willing to correct it? "If you answer "yes" to all of the above questions, the divide the task into small parts and attend to the smallest part with the least effort that you can afford, for the least amount of time that you can afford. Start there. Start small and be sure to motivate yourself by rewarding yourself after the completion of every tiny part of that task. With enough repetition of this process, you will improve your life.

10.   Focus on improving yourself. Align your soul with the Truth, and the Good, and with order and with beauty. Overcome evil, ameliorate suffering, better yourself. Pursue the highest good, and worry not for your sustenance, or for tomorrow, because God will sustain you. Always pay attention to your environment. Tell the truth. Negotiate. Realize that you can be as good as you want to be and that no one is really better off than you. Be humble and patient. Realize that for the solutions to your problems to work, they must be tailored precisely to you and your circumstances. Aim at the highest good. Ask, seek, and knock, but do so fervently, and with conviction and you will be answered; you will find; and the door will be opened unto you. Compare yourself only to the you of yesterday, and not to who another person is today.

KNOWLEDGE CHECK

1. According to Peterson, inside every human being, exists an internal critic, a loud, noisy, innate critical voice that constantly reminds us of our failures and inadequacies and mocks our attempts to rise above the mediocre. Is this true or false? (Check one):
True   [   ]
False   [   ]

2. According to Peterson, there is no equality in human ability or outcome, and there never will be. Is this true or false? (Check one):
True   [   ]

False   [   ]

3. Under Rule 4, Peterson asserts that while we are in this world, we must always navigate towards something better, improved, corrected; that we reside within a framework that conceives the present as eternally insufficient and the future as an eternal opportunity for improvement. And that this is the reason we act at all. Is this true or false? (Check one):
True   [   ]
False   [   ]

4. Under Rule 4, Peterson asserts that people only see what they want to see. And that this is because sight depends on aim, and that aim is a product of value. You see what you aim at and you aim at only those things that you value. In other words, what one wants (what one is intensely focused on) is what one sees nearly to the exclusion of everything else. And this is okay. But it also means that our desires can blind us, our desires can interfere and prevent us from seeing things as they really are. Is this true or false? (Check one):
True   [   ]
False   [   ]

5. Under Rule 4, Peterson teaches that if your life is not going well, perhaps your current knowledge, your idiosyncrasies, your world view, your value structure are blinding you and preventing you from seeing the things you truly need. In that case, your value structure needs some retooling. You need to free yourself from the narrow and concrete confines of your past world view, presuppositions, preconceptions and value structure. You need to let go so that a new world of new possibilities will show itself to you. The fact remains that you can actually lead the world to cooperate with you (or to resist you). If you change what you value (that is what you aim at), you will begin to see new things and the world will begin to present you with new information and reveal to you, things that were previously hidden from you. And then, you can use this new information and new revelations to improve your life. Is this true or false? (Check one):
True   [   ]
False   [   ]

6. Under Rule 4, Peterson states that every human has an internal critic that knows about and mocks all of a person's failures and inadequacies. But Peterson also asserts that this voice of your internal critic is not necessarily wisdom; that it is mere chatter because your "failures and inadequacies" are not your fault. That failures and inadequacies come with the human condition, with Being, as there is no equality in human ability or outcome, and there never will be. He suggests that only delusions/illusions can offer refuge from the angsts of Being and that Being is indeed like a game that has been rigged against you.
(i) Articulate your understanding of what Peterson is saying here. Your writing should provide clear evidence that you understand what he is saying.
(ii) List five significant ways in which the game of life, of living (Being) has been rigged against you?

_____

_____

_____

_____

7. Under Rule 4, Peterson invites us to consider that this game of life which we are playing is somehow rigged. And so he suggests that we stop listening to that critical voice within each of us, that internal critic, and then he further suggests some of the ways by which we can still the voice of that internal critic. Discuss each of the several ways he suggested and express your opinion as to the efficacy of each suggestion.

_____

_____

_____

_____

8. Peterson suggests that standards of "worse or better" are not unnecessary or illusory; that every activity comes with its own internal standards of accomplishment (best, better, good, fair, bad, worse, worst, etc.); that if there was no "better and worse", nothing would be worth doing and there would be no value and, therefore, no meaning, since meaning itself requires the difference between "better and worse".
(i) Articulate your understanding of what Peterson is saying here. Your writing should provide clear evidence that you understand what he is saying.

_____

_____

_____

_____

9. According to Peterson, you have been deceived if you assume that there is just one game or a few games at which to succeed or fail. That is a misconception. Indeed, there are many games in Being and some of these games match your talents. So, if you do not succeed at one, you can try another. In other words, _change the game or invent a new game_. Pick or invent something better matched to your unique mix of strengths, weaknesses and situation.

41

(i) Do you agree or disagree with Peterson on this point?
(ii) Explain your position in writing, in detail.

_____

_____

_____

_____

10. Under Rule 4, Peterson teaches that, indeed, you should pay attention and focus on your physical and psychological environment and fix those things within that environment that bothers you.
(i) How does Peterson suggest that you find out those things within your environment that bothers you, that you may fix.

_____

_____

_____

_____

_____

_____

_____

_____

ACTION STEPS

1. **Under Rule 4, Peterson teaches that inside you and every other human being, exists an internal critic, a loud, noisy, innate critical voice that constantly reminds you of your failures and inadequacies and mocks your attempts to rise above the mediocre.**
(i) Write down the top ten sore points on which you receive the most talk downs, criticism and mockery from your inner voice.
(ii) Articulate a detailed plan of how you intend to address these top ten points.

_____

_____

2. *Peterson also teaches that there is not just one game at which to succeed or fail, that there are many games. And that if you don't succeed at one, you can try another. In other words, that you can change the game or invent a new game.*

(i) Write down a list of the games you are currently playing (e.g. family, profession, education, finances, health, social network, etc.).

(ii) For each game rate your progress from 0% to 100%.

(iii) And for each game, identify three alternatives to that game. Then articulate why you should or should not change to an alternative game.

(ii) Identify and describe a new game that you are able to invent.

(v) If you will change to another game or invent a new game, articulate a detailed plan of how you intend to successfully do so.

3. *Peterson also teaches that you should not compare yourself to others because the specifics of the many games you are playing are so unique to you, that comparison to others is simply inappropriate.*

(i) Compile a list of persons that you habitually compare yourself to and identify in what contexts (games) you make the comparisons.

(ii) For each person on the list above, write down why comparing yourself to that person is self-defeating, unhealthy and inappropriate.

(iii) Articulate a detailed plan of how you intend to eliminate each and every one of those comparisons from your life.

5. Peterson also teaches that gratitude protects you against the feelings of victimhood and resentment.

(i) Do you feel resentment or victimized about anything? Compile a list of those things you feel victimized or resentment about.

(ii) For every item on the list above, articulate why you feel victimized or resentment about that item.

(iii) Articulate a detailed plan of how you intend to address and resolve each and every item of resentment or victimization on the list.

(iv) Do you feel grateful for anything about you? Compile a list of those things you feel grateful about.

(v) For every item on your "grateful list", articulate why you feel grateful about that item.

_____

_____

_____

_____

6. Peterson advocates self-authenticity. He teaches that you should not be afraid to manifest your dark and unspoken desires; stop being afraid and pretending to be moral; stop putting up with things or pretending to like things based only on obligation or because you wish to avoid conflict. In short, be authentic and manifest your true destiny.

(i) Compile a "rap sheet" of your inauthentic self, that is, a list of: (a) your undeclared desires that you have been afraid to manifest; (b) things that you have been pretending to be moral about; (c) things that you are pretending to like but are merely putting up with for one reason or another, etc.

(ii) Articulate a step-by-step plan of how you intend to free yourself from each of these self-imposed points of bondage and become your authentic self.

_____

_____

_____

_____

7. Peterson proposes that to get over your flaws, faults and inadequacies, that you articulate a 3-year plan by which you will work on one adequacy after another (but one at a time), proceeding in small steps and rewarding yourself for every small accomplish towards your goal, until you reach transformative change.

(i) Compile a list of your top ten flaws, faults and inadequacies.

(ii) Articulate a step-by-step, 3-year plan (broken down into 3 annual plans) of how you intend to overcome your top ten flaws, faults and inadequacies.

_____

_____

_____

_____

8. _Peterson also teaches that people only see what they want to see; that sight depends on aim and that aim is only a product of value. Thus that you aim only at those things that you value. The implication of this, therefore, is that the intensity of your desire and your value structure may cause you to become too parochial and too blinded to the rest of what the world has to offer. This is inimical to transformative change because to effect a transformative change, you usually need to jettison your idiosyncratic world view, your current knowledge and your current value structure, so that a new world of new possibilities will reveal itself to you._

(i) Considering the above, examine your values and the things you desire intensely and compile a list of the top twenty values you cherish and things you desire intensely.

(ii) Identify and compile a list of those things that you really need which the above values and desires may be preventing you from realizing, seeing or getting.

(ii) Articulate a step-by-step plan of how you intend to jettison those disabling values and desires of yours (identified in (i) above) so that you may see finally transformative change.

_____

_____

_____

_____

9. _Peterson also admonishes that you should compare yourself only to the you of yesterday, and not to who another person is today. In other words, he suggests that growth is winning and that you win (thus you are a winner) when you grow._

(i) Prepare and present a 500-word written statement to your family and yourself in support of this proposition.

_____

_____

CHECKLIST

[   ] I acknowledge that I have an internal critic that knows all my inadequacies and failures and that always mocks my efforts to rise above mediocrity. But, the voice of this internal critic may not be wisdom. It may not be a meaningful criticism of Being.

[   ] I acknowledge that there is no equality in human ability or outcome and never will be and I am grateful for my own set of strengths and weaknesses.

[   ] I acknowledge that standards of better or worse are not illusory or unnecessary, as every activity comes with its own internal standards of accomplishment.

[   ] I shall still the voice of my internal critic by refusing to accept binary articulations of value. Instead I shall recognize a continuum of value with various degrees and gradations. Nothing is really black and white. There are millions of shades in between.

[   ] I, therefore, acknowledge that there is not just one game at which to succeed or fail in life. There are many games and some of these games match my talents.

[   ] I shall try another game, in case I do not succeed at the one I'm playing. In other words, I shall be ever ready to move, to leave, to quit, to change the game until I find something better matched to my unique mix of strengths, weaknesses and situation. In the event that changing the game does not work, I shall invent a game of my own. The point is that I should be playing only in a game that is matched to my unique mix of strengths, weaknesses and situation.

[   ] I acknowledge that I am playing many games at the same time (career, friends, family, finances, health, personal projects, and miscellaneous pursuits, etc.). I acknowledge that I will most likely perform to varying degrees of success or failure across all these games. But that is how it should be. I do not expect to win at everything!

[   ] I shall not compare myself to others in the various games I am playing. Doing so is inappropriate. I shall remain grateful for what I have, as gratitude protects me against the feelings of victimhood and resentment.

[   ] I shall work hard at becoming adventurous and truthful. I shall always articulate myself, and express what justifies my life. I shall not be afraid to express my dark and unspoken desires. I shall stop putting up with things, or pretending to like things just

because of duty or obligation or because I wish to avoid conflict. I shall stop pretending to be moral.

[   ] I shall, henceforth, take stock of my flaws, faults, imperfections, inadequacies and begin to address them one at a time. I shall proceed in small steps and reward myself as I go. I shall do this for 3 years until my life is transformed.

[   ] I am willing to let go of my idiosyncratic world view, my current knowledge, so that a new world of new possibilities will show itself to me. I acknowledge that this is a vital precondition for transformative change to take place in my life.

[   ] I shall pay attention and focus on my physical and psychological environment and fix those things within my environment that bother me. To fix those things, I shall divide the task into small parts and attend to the smallest part with the least effort. With persistence and repetition, I shall eventually attain lasting change.

[   ] I shall focus on improving myself. I shall align my soul with God, with the Truth and the Good and with order and with beauty. I shall always pursue the highest good, and worry not for my sustenance or for tomorrow, because God will sustain me.

[   ] I shall always tell the truth, be ever ready to negotiate, be humble and patient. I acknowledge that I can be as good as I want to be and that no one is really better off than me and no one can be a better me than me.

[   ] Very importantly, I shall work hard to grow every day and I shall compare myself only to the me of yesterday and not to who some other person is today. This is because growing is winning; to grow is to win!

RULE 5: DO NOT LET YOUR CHILDREN DO ANYTHING THAT MAKES YOU DISLIKE THEM

LESSONS

1. Discipline is important for children and parents should not hesitate to discipline their children where appropriate.

2. The belief that children are perennially innocent is basically naïve and romantic. It is not reality. The reality is that human beings are both evil and good and this innate capacity for good and evil exists in every human being (including children). In other words, children are not perennially good. Thus children should not be left to their own devices, lest the evil overtake the good! Instead they should be properly socialized so that they can become acceptable members of the society.

3. Parents are responsible for teaching children how to behave so that the children can function meaningfully within society. This responsibility is actually an act of mercy based on a long-term judgment.

4. Proper discipline is difficult. It is demanding, and it requires effort. But discipline and punishment are both necessary for the proper training of children. There is no escaping their use.

5. Parents should not (for fear of conflict) avoid correcting their children. A parent must not shirk from disciplinary intervention, merely because such an intervention could be stressful and could bring resentment from the child.

6. It is not true that any form of child discipline is damaging to the child. This ridiculous excuse only serves as a convenient excuse for some parents to shirk their responsibility for disciplining their children.

7. It is also not true that rules can only irreversibly inhibit the creativity of children. This belies the conclusions in scientific literature that limitations and rules actually promote creative accomplishment.

8. It is also not true that it is best to leave children alone, to their own devices, to make their own choices. It is only common sense to note that children are incapacitated in this regard by biological maturity, and that, if left on their own, to make their own

choices, children will mostly make choices that may go against their self-interests in the long run.

9. Also the idea that subjecting children to any adult's dictates (including the dictates of the child's parents) is a sort of oppression and prejudice (like racism, or sexism) is absurd. Shouldn't parents be able to dictate the rules of proper behavior to their children, and train their children so they can become well-adjusted, effective, and successful members of society?

10. Parents may use reward to achieve discipline, by rewarding good behavior in children. This can be very effective. But note that the use of reward to modify behavior can also be very difficult, requiring patience and waiting.

11. Parents may also use both threats and punishment (in appropriate proportions) to help children to learn. In fact, failure to employ these tactics in helping to modify children's behavior is in fact to do harm to children.

12. If parents fail to discipline and train their children properly, the harsher society out there will eventually mete out more severe and painful punishment to those children than the parents could have ever dished out had they not shirked their duty.

13. There is a limited time during which a child can be taught how to behave properly, so time is of the essence. That time is prior to the age of four (4).

14. In disciplining children, parents should keep the rules minimal and relevant. Too many rules can encumber children and cause frustration, so parents should limit the rules.

15. Parents can also use "timeout" to discipline their kids. Time out can be an extremely effective form of punishment

16. Parents can also add physical restraint (where necessary) in disciplining their children.

17. Parents can also apply a swat on the backside to show seriousness. Some situations might call for even more serious actions than those mentioned above.

18. Parents should beware of such clichés as "there is no excuse for physical punishment". This is misguided and nonsensical. Does society itself not physically punish some forms of wrongful behavior? Is jail is not physical punishment? Should physical punishment still be shunned even in those circumstances where it is the only, and fastest means (within reason) to prevent consequence that could quickly turn fatal?

19. Parents should also beware also of the cliché that claims that "hitting a child merely teaches them to hit". This is another misguided and nonsensical idea. In the first

49

place, it is misleading and wrong to describe the normal disciplinary act of a parent in this context as "hitting" and so if it is no hitting, that cliché therefore doesn't even apply.

20.   It should be noted that in order to discipline children appropriately and train them properly, it is better to start off from a two-parent home. Granted that there are other family arrangements, but all forms of family are not all equally viable. Two parents are better for raising children than one parent.

21. Parents should also appreciate their own capacity to be harsh, vengeful, and wicked. So in disciplining their children, parents should adopt an appropriate strategy that can help prevent their darker sides from erupting and taking over. The watchful eye and support of a partner can be helpful in this regard.

22.   Also note that parents are agents for society. And that it is the primary duty of parents to properly bring up and train their children so that they can adapt effectively and productively to society.

23. If parents carry out this duty properly, society will reward their children with opportunity, security, and cooperation. But if parents fail at this duty, society will mercilessly and endlessly mete out severe and painful punishment against their children for the rest of their lives.

24.   So identify those things you like and those that you do not like about your children. And then go to work in correcting those things that you do not like. Keep working on halting all those behaviors and tendencies that you dislike about your children. Persevere and persist because ultimately your efforts will lead to the lifetime happiness, security, and welfare of your children. There are no greater gifts that parents can give to their children than this. So, in a nutshell, just don't allow your kids to do anything that makes you to dislike them

KNOWLEDGE CHECK

1. Under Rule 5, Peterson observes that our society has, for long, been beset by forces bent on deconstructing and reconstructing almost all of society's historically stabilizing values and traditions. He further notes that these forces are vigorously pushing for the dismantling and balkanization of various societal categories supposedly in order to accommodate an increasingly smaller and smaller number of people who will not or do not fit into society's established categories. Peterson rues the fact that these forces call for a social revolution or a cultural restructuring for even the minutest, "peculiarest", individualistic problem.
(i) Identify and describe at least five of the forces in society that you think that Peterson may have been referring to above and state your reasons for concluding that Peterson may have been referring to those forces that your identified.

(ii) Do you think the trend or development that Peterson described above is good for society or bad for society. Articulate your position in detail with copious supporting facts and references.

_____

_____

_____

_____

2. Under Rule 5, Peterson asserts that it is not true that any form of child discipline is damaging to the child.
(i) Outline the argument put forward by Peterson's to support this assertion?
(ii) Do you agree or disagree with him? Articulate your position in detail with copious supporting facts and references.

_____

_____

_____

_____

3. Under Rule 5, Peterson also asserts that it is not true that rules can only irreversibly inhibit the creativity of children.
(i) Outline the argument put forward by Peterson's to support this assertion?
(ii) Do you agree or disagree with him? Articulate your position in detail with copious supporting facts and references.

_____

_____

_____

_____

4. Under Rule 5, Peterson also asserts that it is not true that it is best to leave children alone, to their own devices, to make their own choices.
(i) Outline the argument put forward by Peterson's to support this assertion?
(ii) Do you agree or disagree with him? Articulate your position in detail with copious supporting facts and references.

_____

_____

_____

_____

5. Under Rule 5, Peterson describes the rising idea of adultism. Adultism is the idea that subjecting children to any adult's dictates (including the dictates of the child's parents) is a sort of oppression and prejudice (like racism, or sexism). Discuss adultism, highlighting its merits and demerits.

_____

_____

_____

_____

6. Under Rule 5, Peterson warns parents to beware of such clichés as "there is no excuse for physical punishment".
(i) Outline the argument put forward by Peterson's to support this assertion?
(ii) Do you agree or disagree with him? Articulate your position in detail with copious supporting facts and references.

_____

_____

_____

_____

7. Under Rule 5, Peterson also warns parents to beware of the cliché that claims that "hitting a child merely teaches them to hit".
(i) Outline the argument put forward by Peterson's to support this assertion?
(ii) Do you agree or disagree with him? Articulate your position in detail with copious supporting facts and references.

_____

_____

_____

_____

8. Under Rule 5, Peterson suggests that parents may use both threats and punishment (in appropriate proportions) to help children to learn. He even posits that failure to employ these tactics in helping to modify children's behavior is, in fact, to do harm to children.
(i) Outline the argument put forward by Peterson's to support this assertion?
(ii) Do you agree or disagree with him? Articulate your position in detail with copious supporting facts and references.

_____

_____

_____

_____

ACTION STEPS

1. ***Peterson teaches that discipline is important for children; that parents are responsible for disciplining their children and that when parents discipline their children, it is actually an act of mercy (from parent to child) based on a long-term judgment.***
(i) Prepare and present a convincing 30-minute speech to yourself and your family as to why (a) discipline is important for children, (b) parents are responsible for disciplining their children (c) and parental discipline is actually *an act of mercy* (from parent to child) based on a long-term judgment.

_____

_____

_____

2. ***Peterson provides some tactical guidelines that parents may employ in disciplining their children. These include that parents may: (a) use rewards, (b) threats and punishment (in appropriate proportions), (c) keep the rules minimal and relevant, (d) use the least force necessary, (e) start with the smallest possible intervention, (f) use "timeout" to discipline kids, (g) add physical restraint (where necessary), (h) apply a swat on the***

backside to show seriousness (i) and take more serious actions than those already mentioned (where called for).

(i) Conduct further research on your own and add at least ten (10) additional tactical guidelines for the proper disciplining of children (that is, in addition to the ones already provided here by Peterson).

_____

_____

_____

_____

3. _Peterson notes that if parents discipline and properly train their children, society will eventually reward those children with appreciation, recognition, opportunity, security, cooperation and promotion._

(i) Describe those positive attributes that you believe if you inculcate into your children will eventually cause society to reward them with appreciation, recognition, opportunity, security, cooperation and promotion.

(ii) Write down a step-by-step plan of how you intend to discipline and properly train your children and ensure that those positive attributes are inculcated in them.

_____

_____

_____

_____

4. _But Peterson also warns that if parents fail to discipline and train their children properly, the larger society will eventually, mercilessly and endlessly, mete out more severe and painful punishment to those children for the rest of their lives (much more severe and painful punishment than the parents could have ever dished out, had they not shirked their duty)._

(i) Describe those attributes that you believe that if not inculcated in children _early enough_, may eventually cause society to mete out more severe and more painful punishment on those children.

(ii) Write down a step-by-step plan of how you intend to discipline and properly train your children and ensure that those negative attributes are eliminated from your children's character and habits or are not allowed to take root in your children, in the first place.

_____

5. *Parents who fail to discipline, properly train and socialize their children so as to ensure that they do not become scofflaws, misfits and unacceptable members of society should know that society is waiting to continually and correspondingly punish those children, in future (basically for the negligence of their parents). Some of the ways that society punishes scofflaws, misfits and unacceptable members of the society include: arrest, imprisonment, probation and monitoring, electronic monitoring, inclusion of name on a criminal offenders list, being barred from certain types of employment or from residing in certain areas, loss of civil rights, including the right to vote and the right to own a firearm, community service, civil judgment against the person, fines, restitution, surcharges, loss of driver's license or professional license or any other form of license, deportation or loss of citizenship, forfeiture, impoundment, confiscation, liens on bank accounts, termination from employment, expulsion or suspension from an institution, mandatory substance abuse treatment, mandatory counseling, mandatory completion of a behavioral management program, physical punishment such as flogging and canning (in some countries such as Saudi Arabia and Singapore but not in the USA) and in extreme cases, death penalty aka capital punishment (in some states in the USA).*

(i) Conduct further research on your own and add at least twenty (20) additional ways via which society eventually punishes scofflaws, misfits and unacceptable members of society (basically, people who as children were not disciplined, corrected or properly trained and socialized by their parents to become acceptable members of society).

6. **Certain misconceptions and outright lies surround child discipline. For** *example, it is not true: (a) that any form of child discipline is damaging to the child; (b) that rules can only irreversibly inhibit the creativity of children; (c) that it is best to leave children alone, to their own devices, to make their own choices; (d) that there is no excuse for physical punishment (in child discipline); (e) that "hitting" a child merely teaches the child to*

55

"hit"; that subjecting children to any adult's dictates (including the dictates of the child's parents) is adultism (a sort of oppression and prejudice like racism, or sexism). According to Peterson, these are merely ridiculous assertions that only serve as convenient excuses for some parents to shirk their responsibility for disciplining their children.

(i) Write a statement that explains why all the assumptions above are wrong. You may borrow from Peterson's arguments, but be sure to also add reasoning of your own.

_____

_____

_____

_____

7. Peterson asserts that there is a limited time during which a child can be taught how to behave properly and that such time is prior to the age of four (4).

(i) Does the above statement mean or imply that children older than four (4) years of age can no longer be disciplined or trained on how to properly behave? Explain.

(ii) If you have a child/children who is/are older than four (4) years of age, write down a step-by-step plan of how you intend to continue disciplining and training them despite that they have passed that 4-year window.

_____

_____

_____

_____

8. Peterson also asserts that in order to discipline and train children appropriately, it is better to start off from a two-parent home.

(i) Does the above statement mean or imply that it is not possible to discipline and train children appropriately in other family arrangements? Explain.

(ii) If you have a child/children in a family arrangement other than a two-parent home, write down a step-by-step plan of how you intend to properly and successfully discipline and train the child/children, despite that yours is not a two parent home.

_____

_____

_____

9. *Peterson warns that, in child discipline, parents should also be aware of and beware of their own capacity to be harsh, vengeful, and wicked. So, that in disciplining their children, parents should adopt an appropriate strategy that can help prevent their darker, meaner, evil sides from erupting and taking over.*

(i) Do you (and all human beings) have a darker, evil side? Substantiate your answer to this question in line with Peterson's arguments in Rule 5.

(ii) Write down a step-by-step plan of how you as a parent intend to prevent your darker, meaner, evil side from erupting and taking over in matters of child discipline.

10. **Peterson also observes that parents are agents for society. And that it is the primary duty of parents to properly bring up and train their children so that they can adapt effectively and productively to society.**

(i) Imagine and describe a society where parents have refused to acknowledge and perform their roles as agents of society with respect to disciplining, training and properly socializing children to become acceptable members of society.

(ii) Is the society you described in (i) above a good, desirable society? Articulate your position and substantiate it with cogent reasons.

CHECKLIST

[   ] I acknowledge that discipline is important for children and as a parent I shall not hesitate to discipline my children where appropriate.

[   ] I acknowledge that children are not perennially innocent thus I shall never leave my children to their own devices. Instead, I shall properly discipline, train and socialize my children so that they can become acceptable members of the society.

[   ] I acknowledge that parents are responsible for teaching children how to behave so that the children can function meaningfully within society and that this responsibility is actually an act of mercy (from parent to child) based on a long-term judgment.

[   ] I shall not (for fear of conflict, stress or resentment from my children) avoid correcting or disciplining my children.

[   ] I acknowledge that it is false: (a) that any form of child discipline is damaging to children; (b) that rules can only irreversibly inhibit the creativity of children; (c) that it is best to leave children alone, to their own devices, to make their own choices; (d) that there is no excuse for physical punishment (in child discipline); (e) that "hitting" a child merely teaches the child to "hit"; (f) that subjecting children to any adult's dictates (including the dictates of the child's parents) is adultism (a sort of oppression and prejudice like racism, or sexism). I repudiate and disavow all these false notions.

[   ] I acknowledge that the following tactics are available to me for the purpose of disciplining my children and that I may (using reasonable judgment) employ them or not depending on the circumstances: (a) use of reward, (b) use of threats and punishment (in appropriate proportions), (c) keeping the rules minimal and relevant, (d) use of the least force necessary, (e) starting with the smallest possible intervention, (f) use of "timeout" to discipline kids, (g) use of physical restraint (where appropriate), (h) applying a swat on the backside to show seriousness (i) and taking more serious actions than those already mentioned (where appropriate).

[   ] I acknowledge that if parents fail to discipline and train their children properly, that the larger society will eventually mete out more severe and painful punishment to those children (for infractions and rule violations, etc.) than the parents could have ever dished out to those children had they not shirked their duty of disciplining and properly training their children.

[   ] I acknowledge that my capacity (as a human being) to be harsh, vengeful, and wicked is real. So in disciplining my children, I must adopt an appropriate strategy that will prevent my darker and meaner side from erupting and taking over. My disciplining of my children comes and must come only from a place of overwhelming love and good will.

RULE 6: PUT YOUR HOUSE IN ORDER

LESSONS

1.   There are people who believe that the human reality, the human state of Being is so worthless and so meaningless and that the human race is so contemptible that it deserves to be destroyed. In other words, that the human experience is essentially so insufficient, so unjust, so corrupt and so evil that it rightly deserves to be terminated. This Mephistophelean logic is not uncommon. For some people, their many negative experiences (injustices, victimizations, inequities, chronic sickness, chronic poverty, pain and suffering, etc.) cause them to question the human state of Being, to curse it, and then wish to destroy it.

2.   Indeed, life is hard. Living is hard. Striving to continuously keep one's head above water is hard. And it gets worse because "life sucks and then you die"! Thus the temptation to question the nature of Being becomes ever so compelling. This temptation also arises when we observe from our surroundings some of the seeming incongruities of our Being as humans. Why, for example, do innocent, good people suffer? Why do the guilty and sinful seem to prosper? Why do good men die young and bad men live long? Why do some people suffer wretchedly their whole lives, while others get to live their entire lives in opulent ease and comfort? Why is there so much pain and suffering in this world, anyway? And who or what would you blame for all the pain and suffering that comes with being alive and human? Would you dare to blame God? Or would you blame fate or chance? Or would you blame human flaws, faults, and mistakes? But regardless of where you lay the blame, the most important question is what happens thereafter? What will you do about it?

3.   Well, here is what you should **not** do about it. Do **not** pass judgment on the nature of Being, on life, and then decide to take revenge on Being by destroying life itself.

4.   Instead emulate those people who have emerged from a past of great pain, suffering, and calamity but who have chosen to do good going forward, and not evil? Such people do exist. Indeed, distress at the state of human Being, need not produce nihilism. In fact, you can turn your suffering to fuel for doing good. This is possible because one can understand good (and do good) by experiencing the opposite of good (evil).

5.   Note that vengeance (even seemingly justifiable vengeance) inhibits meaningful, productive thoughts and endeavors (such as cleaning up your act, or working on yourself). So instead of feeling resentful and vengeful against the state of human Being (no matter what grief and misery life may have put you through), jettison the resentment

and the vengefulness so that you may focus on more productive thoughts and endeavors such as working on transforming your life.

6.   When you are suffering, know that such is not exactly out of the earthly norm. After all humans are limited and flawed, and the lived experience of human life is largely tragic. But do not dare blame God. And do not blame nature or reality for the state of human Being. Doing so will only pave way for corruption. It will corrupt your soul.

7.   Instead, examine yourself. Check your ways, and amend them. The fault often is not in the stars, but in us. In any event, do not sulk away in resentment, in self-defeat, and plotting vengeance and destruction (for the real or imagined grievous harm done to you).

8.   If however, your pain, your angst, your suffering has become so terrible and so unendurable that your soul is starting to get corrupted, do the following:

9.   Reassess your life and jettison the negative elements. Change your outlook on things. Cut out your bad habits. Reconsider opportunities. Work harder. Be humble. Choose peace over conflict. Treat your family and friends with respect. Face your responsibilities. Stop engaging in actions or speech that you know are wrong, that are less than honorable, or that disempower you. Do not blame ideology, or any of the many isms, or your enemies, or politicians, or the government, or immigrants, or anyone or anything else. Look to yourself. Order your own life first. In short, start doing things to improve the people and things in your surroundings, your environment, your society, and the world. If you persist in doing this, after a while your lived experience will change, and your life, judgment, happiness, confidence, and fortunes will improve.

10.   So clean up your life, reorganize yourself. Put your own house in perfect order, first, before anything. Become an ambassador for peace and goodness, first. If you do this, then you should expect the world around you to follow your lead and, perhaps, become a better place and perhaps even become a less tragic place. And it is only after you have successfully filled this role, that you would have earned the right to criticize the world. Call yourself to order, first. Put your house in order, first, and the troubles and pains of your world might just begin to melt away.

KNOWLEDGE CHECK

1. Under Rule 6, Peterson discusses some of the suffering and pain of Being that come, not as a consequence of man's personal faults and mistakes, but as events and circumstances that are completely beyond man's control (e.g. death, aging, some diseases, having been born in the first place, etc.). Discuss how Peterson explains these events in relation to the general idea of man's vulnerability and fragility.

_____

_____

_____

_____

_____

2. Peterson observes that there are some people who believe that the human reality or the human state of Being is worthless and meaningless; that the human experience is essentially so insufficient, so unjust, so corrupt, and so evil that it rightly deserves to be terminated and that the human race is so contemptible that it deserves to be destroyed. But Peterson cautions that one should not pass judgment on the nature of Being, on life, and then decide to take revenge on Being by destroying life itself. Instead that one should emulate those people who despite having suffered a past of great pain, suffering and calamity, nevertheless, emerged choosing to do good going forward, rather than evil. Is this true or false? (Check one):
True   [   ]
False   [   ]

3. Peterson teaches that vengeance (even seemingly justifiable vengeance) inhibits other meaningful, productive thoughts and endeavors (such as cleaning up your act, or working on transforming your life). Thus that it is best to jettison the vengefulness so that you may focus on more productive thoughts and endeavors. Is this true or false? (Check one):
True   [   ]
False   [   ]

4. Peterson warns against daring to blame God or nature or reality for your suffering, as doing so will surely corrupt your soul. Is this true or false? (Check one):
True   [   ]
False   [   ]

5. Peterson also teaches that if, however, your pain, your angst, your suffering has become too unendurable such that your soul is starting to get corrupted, then you should reassess your life and discard all negative elements, clean up your life, reorganize yourself, put your own house in perfect order, first, before anything. Cut out your bad habits. Reconsider opportunities. Work harder. Choose peace and goodness, first. And that if you persist in doing this, eventually, your life, judgment, happiness, confidence, and fortunes will change for the better. Is this true or false? (Check one):
True   [   ]
False   [   ]

ACTION STEPS

1. For some people, many negative experiences (injustices, victimizations, inequities) caused them to question the human state of Being, to curse it, and then wish to destroy it.
(i) Have you ever felt this way? If so identify and describe, in writing, the incidents, circumstances or points for which you felt this way.
(ii) Articulate a detailed plan of how you intend to address and resolve these issues in your life.

_____

_____

_____

_____

2. Despite the suffering that life may have put you through, you should still emulate those people who despite having suffered a past of great pain, suffering and calamity, nevertheless, emerged to choose to do good going forward, rather than evil.
(i) Conduct your own research and identify and narrate the stories of five (5) known figures who emerged from pasts of great suffering and calamity, but nevertheless choose to do good rather than evil, going forward.
(ii) Articulate why it is necessary to move on, choosing good over evil, despite that you may have emerged from a past of great suffering and calamity.

_____

_____

_____

_____

3. Thoughts of vengeance (even if seemingly justifiable) are linked to a decreased incidence of meaningful, productive thoughts and endeavors.
(i) Do you agree or disagree with this statement? Articulate your position and substantiate your arguments with copious facts and references.

_____

_____

_____

_____

4. In the event that you are currently suffering, what does Peterson prescribe (a) that you should know, (b) that you should do (c) and that you should never do?

_____

_____

_____

_____

_____

_____

_____

5. And in the event that your pain, your suffering, your angst is currently so terrible and so unendurable that you are beginning to lose your soul to corruption, what does Peterson prescribe that you do so that the troubles and pains of your world may melt away and so that your life, judgment, happiness, confidence, and fortunes may improve?

_____

_____

_____

_____

_____

_____

_____

_____

_____

CHECKLIST

[ ] I shall never permit my negative experiences (injustices, victimizations, inequities) to cause me to question the human state of Being or to curse it or to wish to destroy it.

[ ] I shall never succumb to nihilism, regardless of whatever great suffering that life may have put me through. Instead I shall keep my head up defiantly and emulate those people who despite having suffered a past of great pain, suffering and calamity, nevertheless, emerged to choose to do good, going forward, rather than evil.

[ ] I acknowledge that vengeance (even seemingly justifiable vengeance) inhibits meaningful, productive thoughts and endeavors. I shall, therefore, jettison resentment and vengefulness so that I may welcome more productive thoughts and endeavors such as working on transforming my life.

[ ] In the event that I am currently suffering, then I shall know and acknowledge that suffering is intrinsic in the human condition and that the lived experience of human life is largely tragic. But I shall never, ever dare to blame God. Or to blame nature or reality, as doing so will only end up corrupting my soul.

[ ] In the event that I am currently suffering, I shall instead, examine myself and my ways and amend my faults, as the fault is usually in the human being and not in the stars. I shall not succumb to resentment, self-defeat or self-pity and I shall not succumb to thoughts of vengeance and destruction.

[ ] But in the event that my pain, my angst, and my suffering have become so terrible and so unendurable that I have begun to lose my soul to corruption, I shall reassess my life and discard all negative elements in my life. I shall reorganize myself and put my own house in perfect order, first, before anything. I shall cut out all my bad habits. I shall reconsider past opportunities that I had refused or ignored. I shall work harder. I shall choose peace and goodness, first and disavow conflict and evil. And I acknowledge that if I persist in taking these measures, my life, judgment, happiness, confidence, and fortunes will all eventually change for the better.

[ ] I acknowledge the importance of first calling myself to order, first putting my house in perfect order as a precondition for my world to become a better place with more ease, happiness and improvement than suffering, troubles and tragedy.

[ ] I acknowledge that tragedy, suffering, pain, calamity, stress, sorrow, etc., can all be gone from the human experience, from the human condition, if each individual decides to live right and do good. And so I have made that decision and I shall strive to live right and do good all the days of my life.

RULE 7: PURSUE WHAT IS MEANINGFUL, NOT WHAT IS EXPEDIENT

LESSONS

1.   Life is pain and suffering. That is man's state of Being. Indeed, pain and suffering define the world. But sacrifice (which simply means delayed gratification) can hold both pain and suffering at bay.

2.   Practice and become an expert at sacrificing and sharing. Practice generosity, and life and fortune will always smile at you. Successful people often delay gratification and bargain for a better future (through sacrifice).

3.   God's favor can be gained, and his wrath averted, through proper sacrifice.

4.   The greater the sacrifice, the more effective the sacrifice.

5.   The ultimate sacrifice is of self and/or child.

6.   The greatest possible future and the greatest possible reward that sacrifice can produce is the will of God on earth, the alleviation of suffering on earth, the creation of Heaven on Earth, the advancement of Being, the rectification of the flaws in Being.

7.   The ultimate sacrifice, the greatest sacrifice, which is the sacrifice of self and/or child must be made in order to attain the greatest of all rewards for sacrifice, that is, the greatest of all possible futures, Heaven on Earth and the perfection of Being.

8.   The above therefore means that whoever wants to save the world must make the ultimate sacrifice (of self and child), and of everything they love best and strive to live a life aimed solely at doing the Good. Such a person must abandon expediency, pleasure, and selfishness, and seek only the attainment of ultimate meaning. It is only in this manner that the individual can bring salvation to the world, and advance the state of Being.

9.   Emulate Socrates. Do not lie. Stand by the truth regardless of the circumstances. Allow your conscience to guide you in life. Adhere to the highest ideals. Live properly and do the Good. If you can maintain these standards, security and strength will come to you. You will be noble in every circumstance and you will be able to access and immerse yourself in meaning so deep that even death cannot scare you.

10. Above all, do not tell lies. Lying will condemn your soul to Hell.

11. The assuagement of unnecessary and pointless pain, suffering and misery in this world is an axiomatic good. Treat it as a self-validating and self-evident truth.

12. Always act properly. When you do so, you benefit yourself, everyone around you and the world. When you do so, everything will come together for you, for your good and for the good of the world. You will become meaningfully integrated with the world and its undulations. Life will become more meaningful to you.

13. Do not pursue expedience, and selfish immediate gratification. Expedience is irresponsibility. It is avoiding responsibility. It is superficial, faithless, lacks courage, and it is wrong. Expedience contains no sacrifice and so how can you live a life without sacrifice? Expedience is thoughtless, instant, impulsive unrestrained, parochial and its products are only momentary and short-lived. So shun expedience. Instead, search for, act for/on and aspire only for that which is meaningful.

KNOWLEDGE CHECK

1. Under Rule 7, Peterson discusses "sacrifice" and sacrificing. Fill in the blanks:
(i) Sacrifice can hold _____ and _____ at bay?
(ii) The greater the sacrifice, the _____ the sacrifice?
(iii) The ultimate sacrifice is of _____ or _____?
(iv) The greatest possible future and the greatest possible reward that sacrifice can produce is _____?
(v) _____ must be made in order to attain the greatest of all rewards for sacrifice?
(vi) Whoever wants to save the world must sacrifice _____ and/or _____?
(vii) What is the definition of sacrifice as used by Peterson?
(viii) Discuss self-sacrifice.

2. Peterson teaches that the default human state is intrinsically intertwined with pain and suffering; that such is basically our state of Being; that pain and suffering define this world; but that sacrifice can hold both pain and suffering at bay. Is this true or false? (Check one):
True   [   ]
False   [   ]
3. Peterson also advises that you should make sacrificing and sharing a permanent habit in your life; that if you do so, life and fortune will always smile at you. He also notes that successful people often practice sacrifice. Is this true or false? (Check one):
True   [   ]
False   [   ]

4. Peterson teaches that sacrifice simply means "delayed gratification"; that God's favor can be gained and his wrath averted, through proper sacrifice; that the greater the sacrifice, the more effective the sacrifice; that the ultimate sacrifice is of self and/or child; that the greatest possible reward that sacrifice can produce is the will of God on earth including the alleviation of suffering on earth; that this greatest possible reward requires the greatest sacrifice (of self and/or child); and that whoever wants to save the world must make the ultimate sacrifice (of self and child). Is this true or false? (Check one):

True   [   ]
False   [   ]

5. Peterson also advises that you should emulate Socrates; never lie because lying will corrupt and condemn your soul to Hell; stand by the truth regardless of the circumstances; let your conscience be your guide; adhere to the highest ideals; live properly and do the Good; that by so doing security and strength will naturally come to you, you will be noble in every circumstance and you will benefit yourself, everyone around you and the world. Is this true or false? (Check one):

True   [   ]
False   [   ]

6. Peterson also teaches that the reduction or elimination of unnecessary and pointless pain, suffering and misery in this world is an axiomatic good in and of itself and that you should treat it as a self-validating and self-evident truth. This simply means that you should strive to reduce or eliminate people's unnecessary and pointless pain, suffering and misery; that this, standing alone, is a self-validating good. Is this true or false? (Check one):

True   [   ]
False   [   ]

7. Peterson also warns you against pursuing expedience and selfish, immediate gratification. He suggests that, instead, you should practice sacrifice and search for, act for/on and aspire only for that which is meaningful. Is this true or false? (Check one):

True   [   ]
False   [   ]

ACTION STEPS

1. Under Rule 7, Peterson discusses "sacrifice" and explains that sacrifice simply means "delayed gratification". He also advises that you should practice sacrifice, sharing and generosity, as do many successful people.
(i) The highest sacrifice is of self and/or child for the highest reward, but there are other lower forms of sacrifice that may also suffice for lower rewards. Compile a list of these other lower forms of sacrifice (delayed gratification), that are, nevertheless, vital.

(ii) Articulate your detailed annual plan for incorporating sacrifice, sharing and generosity into your life this year. (note that you should always have a yearly plan for this, in place).

_____

_____

_____

_____

2. Peterson teaches that pain, suffering and tragedy are basically the default human state of Being; but that sacrifice can save you from such calamitous conditions.
(i) Compile a list of the top ten, most egregious points of pain and suffering in your life (they may be physical, material, immaterial or psychological, etc.)
(ii) Articulate a step-by-step plan of how you intend to assuage these points of pains and sufferings through sacrifice. Remember that the greater the sacrifice, the more effective the sacrifice.

_____

_____

_____

_____

3. Peterson also advises you to never lie (instead to stand by the truth regardless of the circumstances); to let your conscience guide you in life; to adhere to the highest ideals; to live properly and to do the Good, always.
(i) Write down these injunctions on a piece of paper, paste the paper on your kitchen wall or on your fridge door and read them every so often.

_____

_____

_____

_____

4. Peterson also teaches that you should strive to reduce or to eliminate people's unnecessary and pointless pain, suffering and misery; and that this, standing alone, is a self-validating good.

(i) Compile a list of ten people who you intend to intervene in their lives this year and reduce or eliminate their pain, suffering and misery as best you can.

(ii) Articulate a step-by-step intervention plan (sponsored and driven by you) that can effectively reduce or eliminate a or some points of pain and suffering from the lives of the individuals identified above.

---

5. Peterson also teaches that God's favor can be gained and his wrath averted, through proper sacrifice.

(i) Do you believe in God? Why or why not? Explain.

(ii) If you believe in God, compile a list of the favors you desire to gain from God.

(iii) Articulate your plan of how you intend to use sacrifice to gain these favors from God.

---

6. Prepare and present a 1000-word statement to your family and yourself on the benefits of sacrifice and the dangers of pursuing expedience and selfish, immediate gratification.

CHECKLIST

[ ] I acknowledge that life is intertwined with pain and suffering; that pain, suffering and tragedy are the human default state of Being. But I shall never succumb to nihilism for that reason, as I equally acknowledge that sacrifice can keep pain and suffering at bay.

[ ] I shall continuously and persistently practice and become an expert at **_sacrificing, sharing and generosity_**. This is because these are bargains for a better future that will most likely cause life and fortune to be kind to me.

[ ] I acknowledge that God's favor can be gained and His wrath averted, through proper sacrifice and so I shall make a habit of sacrifice to God in order to bring me closer to God's grace and blessings.

[ ] I acknowledge that sacrifice simply means "delayed gratification"; that the greater the sacrifice, the more effective the sacrifice; and that the greatest sacrifice is of self and/or child.

[ ] I shall emulate Socrates in that I shall not lie. Instead I shall stand by the truth regardless of the circumstances. I shall always be guided by my conscience and I shall adhere to the highest ideals. I shall live properly and I shall do the Good, for the rest of my life.

[ ] I shall do my best to reduce or eliminate unnecessary and pointless pain, suffering and misery in the lives of specific individuals and in this world. Doing so is an axiomatic good.

[ ] I acknowledge that for me to advance my state of Being, I must abandon expediency, gratuitous pleasure, and selfishness and seek only the attainment of ultimate meaning, the Good, only.

[ ] I shall not pursue expedience and selfish immediate gratification. Expedience is irresponsibility. It is superficial, faithless, lacks courage, and it is wrong. Expedience is thoughtless, instant, impulsive unrestrained and parochial and its products are only momentary and short-lived. Worst of all, expedience contains no sacrifice! So I shall shun expedience. Instead I shall aspire for and seek only that which is meaningful.

[ ] I shall _____

_____

RULE 8: TELL THE TRUTH

LESSONS

1.   Always tell the truth. Even when telling the truth can be harsh and cause momentary discomfort for both you and your audience, nevertheless, tell the truth.

2.   Truth encourages trust, despite (or, more accurately, because of) its seeming harshness.

3.   White lies, or untruths, however well-meant, can produce unintended consequences. Lies distort the substance of Being. It corrupts both the soul and the society alike.

4.   Do not use language to manipulate the world into delivering to you your own false or misrepresented version of reality. It is same as lying. It is just not possible to improve reality through falsification.

5.   When you find yourself in a situation where you don't know what to do or say, just tell the truth.

6.   Take note that choosing to lie or choosing to tell the truth are not just two different choices. They are, indeed, different pathways through life. They are utterly different ways of existing.

7.   Do not try to manipulate reality with words, perception and actions, that is try "to act politically" or to spin reality. Living in this manner is what is known as living a life-lie. Living a life lie weakens your character and your ability to withstand adversity.

8.   A life-lie can also be based on avoidance of confrontation and conflict; hiding in a niche, the routine or the familiar. This type of life-lie robs the individual of vitality, suppresses his/her potentials, yet does not offer any protection from suffering.

9.   Do not avoid and hide. Instead reveal yourself to others. It will also help you to reveal yourself to yourself, so that you may access new information with which to rebuild and renew yourself.

10.   Set your ambitions, even when you are unsure as to what they ought to be. Character development is one of the better ambitions.

11.   Pay attention to your goal and your striving towards it. Attention will give you access to helpful information and help you to progress towards your goal.

12.   Allow reality to inform you as it manifests itself in the present. Welcome the interaction. It will help you to develop ideas as you progress towards your goal.

13.   Your truth is personal and it is only you that can tell it given your unique and peculiar life circumstances. Therefore, understand, articulate and communicate your truth carefully. This will secure you in the present and in the future.

14.   The truth will preserve your soul, and protect you against the buffeting tribulations of life. It will also protect you from yourself. Tell the truth, always, to others, and very importantly, to yourself.

KNOWLEDGE CHECK

1. Under Rule 8, Peterson discusses the "life-lie".
(i) Explain what Peterson means by "life-lie".
(ii) Explain how a "life-lie" can be based on avoidance and discuss the three problems that Peterson identified as associated with this type of life-lie.

_____

_____

_____

_____

2.   Under Rule 8, Peterson advises to lie sometimes, especially when the lie is expedient and will afford you momentary relief or pleasure. Is this true or false? (Check one):
True   [   ]
False   [   ]

3.   Under Rule 8, Peterson teaches that it is okay to tell a white lie or to lie when telling the truth can be harsh and cause momentary discomfort to you and/or your audience. Is this true or false? (Check one):
True   [   ]
False   [   ]

4. Under Rule 8, Peterson teaches that white lies, or untruths, however well-meant, can produce unintended consequences; that lies distort the substance of Being and that they corrupt both the soul and the society alike. Is this true or false? (Check one):

True   [   ]
False   [   ]

5.   Under Rule 8, Peterson teaches to always tell the truth to others and to yourself; that when you find yourself in a situation where you don't know what to do or say, that you should just tell the truth; that truth encourages trust, despite (or, more accurately, because of) its seeming harshness; that the truth will protect you against the buffeting tribulations of life; that it will also protect you from yourself; and that ultimately the truth will preserve your soul. Is this true or false? (Check one):

True   [   ]
False   [   ]

ACTION STEPS

1. Peterson teaches to always tell the truth even when telling the truth can be harsh and cause momentary discomfort to both you and your audience.
(i) Compile a list of the top ten outstanding truths that you have been avoiding to tell because you assume it will cause discomfort to you or your audience.
(ii) Articulate a detailed plan of how you intend to tell these truths regardless of the potential discomfort or pain to you or your audience.

2. Peterson also teaches that white lies, however well-meant, can produce unintended consequences; that lies distort the substance of Being and corrupt both the soul and the society alike.
(i) What are white lies? Are white lies, lies? Explain in line with Peterson's reasoning.
(ii) Compile a list of the white lies you normally tell.
(iii) Articulate the link between lies, the substance of Being, the soul and the society.

3. Peterson also teaches that when you manipulate reality with words, perception and actions (that is, when you spin reality or "act politically"), you lie. You live a lie. You engage in a life-lie, a lie nonetheless.
 (i) What are life-lies? Are life-lies, lies? Explain in line with Peterson's reasoning.
(ii) Describe the impact of a life-lie on the character and abilities of the individual.
(iii) Are you or anyone you know living a life-lie? If your answer is "yes", explain the circumstances and reasons upon which you base your conclusion.

4. Peterson also teaches that when you habitually avoid confrontation and conflict; and/or when you habitually hide yourself in a niche or the routine or the familiar, you also lie. You also live a lie, a life-lie.
(i) Describe the impact of this type of life-lie on the personality, potentials and security of an individual.
(ii) Are you or anyone you know living this type of life-lie? If your answer is "yes", explain the circumstances and reasons upon which you base your conclusion.

5. Peterson also teaches that choosing to lie or choosing to tell the truth are not just two different choices; that, instead they are two diametrically opposed pathways through life with directly opposite effects and consequences. They are utterly different ways of existing.

(i) Articulate your understanding of this statement and compare and contrast the two pathways citing copious examples.

(ii) Based on your answer above, why then must you always tell the truth and never lie regardless of the circumstances or consequences?

CHECKLIST

[　] I acknowledge that telling some truths can be harsh and unpalatable and may cause discomfort to me and or my audience. But, nevertheless, I shall tell the truth regardless of the circumstances or consequences?

[　] I acknowledge that even the so-called white lies (however well-meant) can produce unintended consequences. Lies distort the substance of Being. They corrupt both the soul and the society alike. Therefore, I shall not tell lies (even the so-called white lies).

[　] I acknowledge that using language, words, actions or perceptions to manipulate the world into delivering to me, my own false or misrepresented version of reality is the same as lying. Spinning reality is also the same as lying and lying does not improve reality, so I shall not engage in such an act. I shall not lie.

[　] I shall tell the truth at all times. Even when I find myself in a situation where I don't know what to do or say, I shall simply tell the truth.

[　] I shall not base my life on deceit and misrepresentation or "acting politically" or spinning reality. Living in this manner is living a life-lie and living a life-lie weakens character and the ability to withstand adversity.

[　] I shall not avoid confrontation/conflict, or hide in a niche, or in the routine, or in the familiar. Living in such a manner is also living a type of life-lie that robs the individual of vitality and suppresses potentials, yet does not offer any protection from suffering.

[　] I shall reveal myself to others, instead of avoiding and hiding. Doing so will give me access to new information with which to rebuild and renew myself.

[　] Most importantly, I shall always reveal myself to myself. I shall never hide myself from myself.

[　] I acknowledge that the truth will preserve my soul and protect me against the vagaries, tribulations and tragedies of life. It will also protect me from myself. I shall, therefore, always tell the truth to others and, very importantly, to myself.

RULE 9: ASSUME THAT THE PERSON YOU ARE LISTENING TO MIGHT KNOW SOMETHING YOU DON'T

LESSONS

1.   True thinking can be very difficult. If you aren't very good at thinking, the next best thing is to talk. Talking can facilitate thinking.

2.   But if you have to talk, then you would need someone to listen to you. Unfortunately, many of us do not know how to listen.

3.   If you can listen, people will generally tell you everything in their heads.

4.   Good listening can transform people.

5.   Listening to people can also help you to improve your own life. From listening, you can learn from the experience and mistakes of others.

6.   Approach each conversation as if the conversation is a special and valuable opportunity for you to learn something new.

7.   A good conversation should not be a trophy piece in an underlying contest for power and dominance between the participants. A good conversation is not a WWE wrestling bout. Distorting a conversation for such underhanded ends is a crime against conversation.

8.   A good conversation should not be a monologue. The offloading of one participant's stream of consciousness upon the other, is also a crime against conversation.

9.   A good conversation requires the mental presence of the participants (attention). The physically present, but absent-minded conversationalist is no conversationalist. That is also a crime against conversation.

10.   A good conversation requires a mental give and take and the shifting of positions (where called for). A stubborn conversationalist who is adamant, and who refuses to

recognize, and stubbornly disregards the very point of the conversation is guilty of a crime against conversation.

11.   One good technique that promotes effective listening is to summarize the other party's speech/message. This technique forces you to (i) understand the message from the other party (ii) stick to the issue, the crux of the matter; (iii) avoid strawman arguments. It also provides the other party with the opportunity of correcting any misunderstandings.

12.   Listen, to yourself and to those with whom you are speaking. As you do so, you would be continually learning. There are plenty nuggets of information, truth and wisdom to be found in conversation, in listening. Always assume that the person you are listening to might have some of those nuggets to deliver to you. So pay attention and listen.

KNOWLEDGE CHECK

1. Under Rule 9, Peterson suggests one good technique that promotes effective listening. He also outlines the advantages of this technique.
(i) Discuss that technique suggested by Peterson.
(ii) Outline the advantages of that technique as suggested by Peterson.

_____

_____

_____

_____

2. According to Peterson, *talking can facilitate thinking*. Is this true or false? (Check one):
True   [   ]
False   [   ]

3. According to Peterson, *if you can listen, people will generally tell you everything in their heads*. Is this true or false? (Check one):
True   [   ]
False   [   ]

4. Under Rule 9, Peterson teaches that listening to people can help you to improve your life, because from listening to people, you can learn from their experience and mistakes; therefore, that you ought to approach each conversation as if the conversation is a special and valuable opportunity for you to learn something new. Is this true or false? (Check one):

True   [   ]
False   [   ]

5.   A good conversation is neither a contest for power and dominance between the participants; nor is it a monologue. It requires the mental presence (attention) and mental exchange (including the shifting of positions where necessary) of the participants. Is this true or false? (Check one):
True   [   ]
False   [   ]

6. According to Peterson, all conversations are not equal and never assume that there is something to learn from every conversation. Therefore, you should pick and choose those who you should listen to and simply ignore the rest. Is this true or false? (Check one):
True   [   ]
False   [   ]

ACTION STEPS

1. Peterson teaches that listening to people can help you to improve your life; that this is because from listening to people, you can learn from their experience and mistakes; that you ought to approach each conversation as if the conversation is a unique opportunity for you to learn something new and that if you can listen, people will generally tell you everything in their heads.
(i) Compile a list of the twenty benefits of good listening skills.
(ii) Reflect deeply and then write down the many ways in which listening to other people has improved your life.

_____

_____

_____

_____

2. Under Rule 9, Peterson identifies a few "crimes against conversation".
(i) Identify and describe these "crimes against conversation".
(ii) Conduct further research and identify other "crimes against conversation".

_____

_____

_____

_____

3. Practice summarizing the speech/message of at least 5 participants with whom you engage in conversation during the day, every day.

_____

_____

_____

_____

4.   One good technique that promotes effective listening is to summarize the other party's speech/message. This technique forces you to (i) understand the message from the other party (ii) stick to the issue, the crux of the matter; (iii) avoid strawman arguments. It also provides the other party with the opportunity of correcting any misunderstandings.

_____

_____

_____

_____

5.   Listen, to yourself and to those with whom you are speaking. As you do so, you would be continually learning. There are plenty nuggets of information, truth and wisdom to be found in conversation, in listening. Always assume that the person you are listening to might have some of those nuggets to deliver to you. So pay attention and listen.

_____

_____

_____

_____

[   ] I acknowledge that true thinking can be very difficult but that through talking, I can facilitate my thinking.

[   ] I acknowledge that I need to improve my listening skills; that I can learn a lot from people, from their experiences and their mistakes (just by listening to them attentively); that indeed, every conversation is a special and valuable opportunity for me to learn something new; so that listening to people can help me to improve my life. Therefore, I shall henceforth listen attentively to anyone with whom I am engaged in conversation.

[   ] I respect the honor, value and opportunity in a conversation, therefore, I shall not pervert a conversation into a struggle for power and dominance or into a monologue dominated by me or become inattentive to the conversation.

[   ] I shall henceforth make a habit of summarizing the speech/message of the party with whom I am engaged in conversation, as I acknowledge that doing so facilitates the way for a good conversation.

[   ] I shall henceforth also make a habit of listening to myself so as to be in tune and in peace with my Being.

[   ] I shall henceforth assume that the person I am listening to has some rare nuggets of information, truth, wisdom and opportunity to deliver to me.

[   ] Indeed, I acknowledge that, generally, people will tell one everything in their heads, if only one can listen attentively and patiently.

[   ] I also acknowledge that good listening/ good conversation can transform people because it is an opportunity and a platform for the mutual exchange of respect, goodwill, truth, wisdom and empowering information and opportunities.

[   ] So, again, I shall henceforth listen attentively, patiently and respectfully to whoever I am conversing with.

RULE 10: BE PRECISE WITH YOUR SPEECH

LESSONS

1.   Precision and the specific identification of things, extricates things from their macrocosm, from their interconnectedness with everything else, and presents them to you as viable objects, obedient to your values, meanings and utility. Precision simplifies things.

2.   Therefore be precise. Do not leave things vague, If you do, everything will conflate into everything else. And this can make the world too confusing and too complex to handle.

3.   Again, precision specifies. It separates the wheat from the chaff or this bushel of wheat from that bushel of wheat. Precision may deliver the bad news, but it will be kind enough to give you an honest assessment.

4.   Mind what you tell yourself and others. Find the appropriate words, the precise words before you speak to yourself or to others.

5.   Do not shrink away and hide, avoid or tolerate imprecision. Engage with it as soon as it materializes. Correct it. If you ignore it, it will eventually grow to monstrous, uncontrollable proportions.

6.   Precise, forthright and truthful words will sanitize your reality transforming it into a well-ordered, well-defined, simple, easy, comfortable and habitable reality. Precise speech conjures order and habitability from an otherwise chaotic world.

7.   Even in conversation, define the topic of the discourse and stick to it. Do this even for difficult conversations. If you do not do this, the conversation will become about everything else. Be precise in your conversation.

8.   Be precise in your plans, your objectives, your goals, and your ambition. Do this because without precision you are unlikely to attain them. Imprecision and randomness amount to no particular direction. It is tantamount to wandering purposelessly. What can you achieve in life in this manner?

9.   Be precise in words and deed. It is better to say what you mean. And then act on what you said. That way (depending on what happens) you can discover any error in your meaning, and the opportunity to correct such errors. And it may well be that you may also discover that your original meaning, thoughts and actions, were indeed correct. This

is how you can discover meaning in your life, meaning which can protect you from tragedy.

10.   Being is chaotic, but confront it. Life is difficult, but engage it. Dive in and push ahead, but let precision be your guide. Be precise in your daily tasks and aims, and in your overall life goals and ambition. Be precise in your speech to keep chaos of Being at bay.

KNOWLEDGE CHECK

1. Under Rule 10, Peterson discusses precision in speech.
(i) Discuss the merits and benefits of precision based on Peterson's arguments.
(ii) Discuss the link between precision and chaos based on Peterson's arguments.

_____

_____

_____

_____

_____

_____

2. According to Peterson, precision simplifies things. It de-groups things, isolates them and presents them independently on their own, so then you are able to process and understand them as viable or not viable in accordance with your values, preferences and meanings. Is this true or false? (Check one):
True   [   ]
False   [   ]

3. According to Peterson, precision sanitizes reality. It introduces order, definition, clarity and habitability to reality, thus transforming an otherwise chaotic world into a well-ordered, well-defined, simple, easy, comfortable and habitable space. Precision specifies and compartmentalizes. It is honest in delivery. Indeed, precision is truth. Is this true or false? (Check one):
True   [   ]
False   [   ]

4.   Being is chaotic. But precision can tame or keep the chaos of Being at bay. Is this true or false? (Check one):
True   [   ]
False   [   ]

ACTION STEPS

1. Peterson teaches that you should be precise and not leave things vague; that when you leave things vague, everything conflates into everything else thus making the world too confusing and too complex to handle.

(i) Compile a list of the things, issues or areas of your life about which you are intentionally or unintentionally vague.

(ii) Write down the benefits that may accrue to you if you were to become precise about those items on the above list.

(iii). Articulate your plan of how you intend to bring precision to those items identified in the list mentioned in (i) above.

_____

_____

_____

_____

2. Peterson also teaches that you should be careful about what you tell yourself and others; that you should find and choose the appropriate words, the precise words before you speak to yourself or to others.

(i) Is there a difference between the benefits/justification for being precise to yourself as opposed to being precise to others? Explain in detail.

(ii) Articulate what you must do every day in order to remind/compel yourself to become precise to yourself and to others, until it becomes a permanent habit of yours.

_____

_____

_____

_____

_____

_____

_____

[   ] I acknowledge that precision simplifies things and that precision brings order, definition, clarity and habitability to my world.

[   ] I shall henceforth, therefore be precise and not leave things vague.

[   ] I shall henceforth mind what I tell myself and others and I shall use only appropriate and precise words in speaking to myself and to others.

[   ] I shall henceforth not hide from, avoid or tolerate imprecision in my life. I shall engage with it and correct it whenever it materializes in my life. I shall never ignore it.

[   ] I shall henceforth be precise in my conversations (even the difficult conversations). This means that I shall define or acknowledge the topic of each conversation and stick to that topic without deviating.

[   ] I shall henceforth be precise in my plans, objectives, goals and ambition, as doing so makes it more likely that I may achieve them.

[   ] I shall henceforth be precise in my words and deeds because precision in speech and actions is a pathway through which I can discover meaning in my life and protect myself from tragedy.

RULE 11: LEAVE CHILDREN ALONE WHEN THEY ARE SKATEBOARDING

LESSONS

1.   Boys can engage in some brave but dangerous physical activities, some of which may even be considered stupid. But such activities offer them the opportunity to attempt to triumph over danger, to face fear and doubt and to overcome them. Overprotection negates this attribute. Overprotection (especially of children) prepares them for failure when faced with danger in the future.

2.   Thus the instituting of measures to overprotect kids and bar them from facing reasonable danger is ultimately against human development. Beware, such measures (and the ideologies that support them) are essentially motivated by a deep and destructive anti-human spirit.

3.   This anti-human spirit has permeated our universities. Loud voices against "oppression" can now be heard all over our universities. Whole disciplines have now become skewed against men and now, by default, treat men as guilty and men's activities as dangerous.

4.   These universities also encourage direct radical political activities by their students in furtherance of particular political agendas, yet they receive public funding. Why?

5.   These universities indoctrinate their students with baseless anti-human theories concerning the relationship between men and women, and the nature of hierarchy! They teach the destruction of our culture, yet they receive public funding. Why?

6.   The patriarchy is not proof of men's oppression of women; instead, it was a collective attempt by both men and women, over millennia, to free each other from the suffering, death, disease and drudgery that marked life in the not-too-distant past, to gain freedom from certain vulnerabilities. Nature (not men) is the primary source of the oppression of women. Indeed, historically men have been partners and supporters of women (not oppressors).

7.   Absolute equality, everywhere, and in everything may not be possible, and may not be attainable. It would necessitate the sacrifice of value, itself? A complex, successful culture, instead, allows for many games, many players, and many types of wins and successes at the many games by many of the players of the many games within that culture. It celebrates competence, skill and ability, not some utopian, impractical, and ultimately unjust notion of absolute equality. Is this not better?

8.   The world will not be better if boys were brought up like girls (feminized) to reduce their aggressive tendencies. Aggression is not merely learned. It is innate. It is another side of determination. And it is good for human development.

9.   Beware the spirit that objects when boys are trying to become men. That is not a friendly spirit. It is an antihuman spirit. It does not mean well for boys, for men, or for women for that matter. No human being who supports the interests of humanity should identify or ally herself or himself with such a thing.

10.   So do not disturb children when they are skate-boarding. They'll tumble and fall and scrape, but they would have also engaged, learnt and toughened up. And that is a good thing.

KNOWLEDGE CHECK

1 (i) Describe the activities of the "anti-human spirit" in society as highlighted by Peterson under Rule 11.
(ii) Should universities that promote direct radical political activities by their students in furtherance of particular political agendas receive public funding? Explain your position in detail.

_____

_____

_____

_____

2. Under Rule 11, Peterson discusses the patriarchy and suggests that the patriarchy is not proof of men's oppression of women; but that instead it is a collective attempt (ongoing for millennia) by both women and men to unchain themselves from the shackles of the suffering, drudgery, disease, and death that characterized life in the past, not too long ago. He further suggests that nature (not

men) is the primary source of the oppression of women, and that historically men have been partners and supporters of women (not oppressors of women). Do you agree or disagree with Peterson? Outline your argument in detail.

_____

_____

_____

_____

3. According to Peterson *instituting measures to overprotect kids and bar them from facing reasonable danger is ultimately against human development*. Do you agree or disagree with Peterson? Outline your argument in detail.

_____

_____

_____

_____

4. According to Peterson *absolute equality, everywhere and in everything, is* utopian, impractical, unattainable and even impossible. *It would necessitate the sacrifice of value and is ultimately unjust.* Do you agree or disagree with Peterson? Outline your argument in detail.

_____

_____

_____

_____

5. According to Peterson *the world will not be better if boys were brought up like girls (feminized) in order to reduce their aggressive tendencies. Aggression is not merely learned. It is innate. It is another side of determination. And it is good for human development.* Do you agree or disagree with Peterson? Outline your argument in detail.

_____

_____

ACTION STEPS

1. Peterson teaches that boys can engage in some brave but dangerous physical activities, some of which may even be considered stupid; but that such activities offer them the opportunity to attempt to triumph over danger, to face fear and doubt and to overcome both; therefore, that overprotection of children negates this attribute and prepares children for failure when faced with danger in the future.

(i) If you agree with Peterson, articulate the guidelines you will follow in allowing your children to engage in those physical activities that may even be described as "dangerous and stupid", yet brave, didactic and in the best interest of children, according to Peterson.

(ii) If you have been overprotecting your children, write a statement detailing how and in what areas you have been overprotecting them and articulate a plan of how you intend to decrease or eliminate your overprotection.

_____

_____

_____

_____

2. Peterson teaches that we should beware of the spirit that objects when boys are trying to become men; that such is not a friendly spirit; that it is an antihuman spirit that does not mean well for boys, for men (or even for women for that matter); and that no human being who supports the interests of humanity should identify or ally herself or himself with such a thing.

(i) If you agree with Peterson, then, articulate a step-by-step plan of how you intend to raise your boys to become men.

(i) If you disagree with Peterson, then, articulate a step-by-step plan of how you intend to raise your boys in avoidance of gender stereotypes.

_____

_____

_____

_____

CHECKLIST

[   ] I acknowledge that overprotection robs children of the opportunity of developing important life skills that would enable them to face danger and defeat fear and doubt later on in their lives. Overprotection prepares children for failure when faced with serious challenges in the future.

[   ] I shall henceforth, therefore not overprotect my children.

[   ] Because I agree with Peterson, I shall raise my boys to become men.
OR
[   ] Because I disagree with Peterson, I shall raise my boys without inculcating any gender stereotypes in them. (*Cancel whichever does not apply*)

[   ] I shall not disturb children when they are skate-boarding (or engaging in some brave but minimally "dangerous" physical activity). I acknowledge that they'll tumble and fall and scrape, but then, they would have also engaged, learnt, toughened up and prepared themselves to be able to face and overcome danger and serious challenges in the future. And that is a good thing.

RULE 12: PET A CAT WHEN YOU ENCOUNTER ONE ON THE STREET

LESSONS

1.   Life is suffering. Human beings are intrinsically fragile, breakable, vulnerable, and destructible. This is the human reality, the human condition, our state of Being.

2.   Limitations. Vulnerability. Fragility. These give impetus to human existence. These are the immutable conditions of Being. These are what make us human.

3.   Being requires Becoming, and Becoming implies "to become more". Thus, Becoming can only be possible coming out of a situation of limitation. Perhaps this is why Being and limitation are so inexorably linked.

4.   Despite that life does indeed inflict much pain and suffering on humans, that still does not justify hatred of Being. Such thinking holds no goodness in it. It merely desires to inflict suffering for its own sake. It is evil.

5.   To understand why pain and suffering exist in this world you need to know that Being and suffering and M&Ms come together (a trio). M&Ms are "magical moments", those magical and wonderful moments of private joy when all your pain and suffering are alleviated, albeit momentarily or for the short-term).

6.   Being human requires imperfection (limitations, vulnerabilities, fragilities, including pain and suffering). Limitations are human.

7.   But you may notice that a human being generally loves another human being because of that other person's limitations, their vulnerabilities.

8.   Perfection (that is, Being without the limitations) is boring. It is specific in nothing. It strives for nothing. It is nothing. That is certainly not being human.

9.   There seems to be a point beyond which humans cannot, and might not want to go in their quest for improvement. Perhaps this is because to go beyond that point is to sacrifice our humanity, to break the imperfection barrier and to finally become perfect. And when we do that we are no longer human. We become something else.

10.   This is a wonderful life, despite its many thorns! This is indeed a beautiful life, after all! Enjoy its many beautiful, magical moments. Celebrate the wonder of Being. It is in these small but magical moments that Being itself offers you the means by which to cope with all that suffering and pain that accompanies Being.

11.   So, pet a cat when you run into one in the street. Enjoy life's little pleasures!

KNOWLEDGE CHECK

1. Under Rule 12, Peterson discusses Being, suffering and M&Ms.
(i) What are M&Ms as described by Peterson under Rule 12?
(ii) Why do Being, suffering and M&Ms come together? Link Being, suffering and M&Ms to Peterson's explanation in chapter 1 of the fundamental binary categorization of order and chaos, and male and female.
(iii) Considering Peterson's arguments under Rule 12, explain in detail why you should pet a cat when you run into one in the street (metaphorically speaking).

_____

_____

_____

_____

2. Peterson teaches that Being requires Becoming, and that Becoming implies "to become more". Thus, that Becoming can only be possible coming out of a situation of limitation and that, perhaps, this is why Being and limitation are so inexorably linked.
(i) Articulate in writing your understanding of the above proposition. Your writing should contain sufficient evidence that you thoroughly understand what Peterson is talking about in the above proposition.

_____

_____

_____

_____

3. According to Peterson, despite that life inflicts too much pain and suffering on humans, that still should not justify hatred of Being. Such thinking that holds a seeming justification for hatred of being holds no goodness in it. It merely desires to inflict suffering for suffering's sake. It is therefore evil. Is this true or false? (Check one):

True   [ ]
False   [ ]

4. According to Peterson, to understand why pain and suffering exist in this world you need to know that Being and suffering and M&Ms come together (a trio); that M&Ms are "magical moments" (that is, those magical and wonderful moments of private joy when all your pain and suffering are alleviated, albeit momentarily or for the short-term); that it is in those small but magical moments that Being itself offers you the means by which to cope with all that suffering and pain that accompanies Being. Is this true or false? (Check one):

True   [ ]
False   [ ]

5. Peterson also teaches that there is an imperfection barrier (which is that point beyond which humans cannot and might not want to go in their quest for improvement); that, perhaps, this is because to go beyond the imperfection barrier is to sacrifice our humanity and to finally become perfect; and that when we do that, we are no longer human, instead we become something else; that being human requires imperfection (limitations, vulnerabilities, fragilities, including pain and suffering); and that limitations are human while perfection is not human. Is this true or false? (Check one):

True   [ ]
False   [ ]

ACTION STEPS

1. Peterson also teaches that life is suffering; that human beings are intrinsically fragile, breakable, vulnerable, and destructible; that limitations, vulnerability and fragility are the immutable conditions of Being; that these are what make us human; and that this is the human reality, the human condition, the human state of Being.
(i) Considering the above, describe what you currently do to keep the pain and suffering described above at bay
(ii) Articulate a detailed plan of what you *should* do to keep the pain and suffering of Being at bay.

---

2. Finally, after all is said and done, this is a wonderful life (despite its many thorns)! This is indeed a beautiful life! And Peterson teaches that you should make sure you enjoy the M&Ms that come with life. (M&Ms are those event-triggered magical and wonderful

moments of private joy when all your pain and suffering are alleviated, albeit momentarily).

(i) Compile a list of the recurrent M&Ms in your life.

(ii) Articulate a plan of how you intend to incorporate more of these M&Ms into your life on a daily basis.

CHECKLIST

[   ] I acknowledge that life is suffering; that human beings are intrinsically fragile, breakable, vulnerable, and destructible; that limitations, vulnerability and fragility are the immutable conditions of Being; that these are what make us human; and that this is the human reality, the human condition, the human state of Being.

[   ] I shall not succumb to despair, despondency or hatred and contemplate the destruction of Being or curse Being (despite the pain, suffering, limitations and vulnerabilities of Being). Instead I shall employ truth, precision, responsibility, accountability, sacrifice, meaning and M&Ms to keep the limitations of Being at bay.

[   ] I acknowledge that being human implies imperfection, limitation, vulnerability fragility, etc. But I also acknowledge that the existence of limitation and vulnerability in one human triggers love for that human from another human. So, it may not be entirely bad to be limited and vulnerable. I accept my vulnerabilities. Perfection is not being human.

[   ] This is a wonderful life, a beautiful life (despite its many thorns)! I shall make sure that I enjoy my life and the many M&Ms that come with it! I shall celebrate the wonder of Being. So, I shall enjoy life's little pleasures from this day forward!!!

APPENDIX A: CERTIFICATE OF COMMITMENT

CERTIFICATE
OF
COMMITMENT

I, _____,

HEREBY COMMIT MYSELF TO LIVING IN ACCORDANCE WITH THE PRINCIPLES AND GUIDELINES CONTAINED IN THE BOOK, "**12 RULES FOR LIIFE: AN ANTIDOTE TO CHAOS**" BY DR. JORDAN B. PERTERSON,

SIGNATURE: _____

DATE: _____

WITNESS: _____

APPENDIX B: THE MASTER CHECKLIST

This is a master checklist of all the action items and important points in the book. Review this master checklist every day and ensure that your thoughts and activities are in line with its prescriptions. Some items on the list are repeated on purpose. Consider that as an indication of their extra importance and just get to working and living this master checklist. It's pleasantly challenging and it's fun. You can do it! Let's go!

RULE 1: STAND UP STRAIGHT WITH YOUR SHOULDERS BACK

[   ] I acknowledge that territory matters and that social status matters too. In fact, as much as territory matters, social status also, almost equally matters. Both are extremely vital for survival.

[   ] I shall take daily steps (even if micro steps) to establish or maintain enough dominance within my territory to enable me to survive and to live in social harmony with other co-inhabitants in my territory.

[   ] I acknowledge that throughout nature, abilities within and among the species are not equal. And that those with stronger or more abilities control more of the available resources. Thus, I shall take daily steps to develop myself and increase my abilities.

[   ] I acknowledge that negotiating or maintaining a social status (a position within the dominance hierarchy in any given territory) is characteristically fraught with great difficulties (which are more or less inevitable). I am not intimidated by those difficulties.

[   ] I acknowledge that phased confrontation is one way to renegotiate or maintain one's position on the dominance hierarchy. But it is not the only way. Other attributes are important including forming beneficial alliances with loyal subordinates and paying attention to and cooperating with the females and the young. I shall come up with a step-by-step plan and take daily steps towards forming beneficial alliances within my territory, paying attention to and cooperating with the females and the young within my territory.

[   ] I acknowledge that the dominance hierarchy or negotiating a good position within it is not Machiavellian or evil. This is because the dominance hierarchy is natural. It has existed for a long time (approximately 500 million years). And it has been selected by

nature for eons. It has impacted life on earth for eons thus it is "natural", ancient, real and permanent.

[   ] I acknowledge the importance of serotonin. It governs posture and it impacts positioning within the dominance hierarchy. And higher levels (not lower levels) of serotonin are more desirable.

[   ] I shall boost my serotonin levels via eating a healthy, pro-serotonin diet, exercising regularly, getting enough sunshine or light therapy, getting a massage from time to time, avoiding stress, maintaining a positive outlook and maintaining a healthy microbiome.

[   ] I acknowledge that the dominance calculator can be disrupted or distorted. Thus I shall avoid all negative habits that can lead to that end including (i) positive feedback loops, (ii) addiction to alcohol or drugs (iii) anxiety disorder - e.g. agoraphobia, (iv) depression, (v) and isolation, etc.

[   ] I also acknowledge that the dominance calculator can sometimes, malfunction. To prevent this, I shall take steps to incorporate predictability and routine in my daily activities. I shall make effort to automatize my daily activities.

[   ] I shall wake up from sleep every morning early (no later than 6AM) regardless of what time I went to bed the night before.

[   ] I shall ensure that my breakfast contains enough protein and healthy fats and that I eat breakfast early (as soon as you wake up).

[   ] I shall henceforth be and act like the WINNER-LOBSTER. I shall henceforth fix my posture, stand up straight, pull my shoulders back and walk with confidence. I shall demand more respect and fair treatment from others. I shall henceforth live with panache and aplomb.

[   ] I shall henceforth no more act like a LOSER-LOBSTER. Never again shall I slouch, sulk, avoid eye contact, disappear at the first sign of conflict, or engage in any other mannerisms or allow any other appearances that convey defeat, subordination and low status to others!

[   ] I am a winner because I said so. I am the WINNER-LOBSTER because I said so. And I shall henceforth live every day of my life as the winner that I am. I am worthy of respect, belonging, loving and being loved. And I am enough in every respect (despite whatever imperfections and vulnerabilities that I may have). My imperfections and vulnerabilities are irrelevant. I am still a winner because I said so. I am still the WINNER-LOBSTER because I said so.

RULE 2: TREAT YOURSELF LIKE SOMEONE YOU ARE RESPONSIBLE FOR HELPING

[ ] I shall not indulge in self-loathing (despite man's original sin and the subsequent fall of man. I am not naked, ugly, wicked, disloyal, disobedient, worthless, cowardly or dishonorable. I have been redeemed by the grace of God.

[ ] I acknowledge that the way forward now is to work on improving myself to earn my place besides God, again. In all my thoughts, words and deeds I shall strive for virtue and the good.

[ ] I acknowledge that virtuous self-sacrifice is good. But I shall not take it too far. I shall not allow myself to be victimized, or abused or to be turned into a slave for the interest of others. There is no virtue in that.

[ ] I acknowledge that I have an obligation to my family, friends and others outside of yourself to take good care of myself and I shall henceforth never cease to take good care of myself, love myself and treat myself with respect and kindness, always.

[ ] I acknowledge that there is a spark of God in me which does not belong to me, but to God alone, thus that I am a vessel that contains a quantity of God. I, therefore, acknowledge that it is my obligation to take good care of me (God's vessel) and I shall henceforth never cease to take good care of myself, love myself and treat myself with respect and kindness, always.

[ ] I shall not subject myself or allow anyone to subject me to any kind of maltreatment or abuse.

[ ] If I see any signs or symptoms of ill health in me, I shall seek medical intervention immediately. If I am prescribed medication, I shall fill my prescriptions and take my medication faithfully, as directed.

[ ] I shall always consider the future and make good plans for my career, health, family, finances, spirituality etc.; and work my plans, diligently, for a prosperous future.

[ ] I shall articulate, by myself, my own vision and principles in life and define my own identity, so as to have a clear direction in my life and to guard against being taken advantage of. And I shall hang on to my vision, principles and direction in life for a purposeful and fulfilling life.

[ ] I shall make my life choices very carefully in order to articulate my Being.

[ ] I shall not allow myself to succumb to indiscipline. Instead I shall pursue a course of self-discipline.

96

[　] I shall that I keep all my promises, especially those That I make to myself.

[　] I shall always reward myself for my accomplishments (great or small) so as to motivate myself and build trust with myself.

[　] I shall exercise great care in how I act towards myself, and I shall ensure that I act towards myself only in ways that are likely to guide me towards becoming a good person.

[　] I shall invest in my personal growth and in improving my personality
Improve your personality.

[　] I shall devote my life to making the world a better place and I shall start by strengthening the individual, starting with myself.

[　] I shall devote my life to making the world a better place and I shall start by strengthening the individual, starting with myself.

[　] I shall strive always to bring myself closer to God.

RULE 3: MAKE FRIENDS WITH PEOPLE WHO WANT THE BEST FOR YOU

[　] I shall make only those friendships that will improve your life. I shall review my life, henceforth, and continue only with those friendships that improve my life.

[　] I shall never have a low opinion of yourself. I understand and acknowledge that I deserve better. Indeed, I deserve the best.

[　] I acknowledge that I am responsible for creating my own world by myself with the tools I have at hand I shall create and maintain my best world for myself.

[　] I shall avoid associating with losers

[　] I shall avoid attempting to rescue a habitual loser, noting that not every loser is a victim and not every loser wishes to be rescued or saved.

[　] I acknowledge that I have no moral obligation to make friends with, or to support, or to rescue a habitual loser.

[　] I understand that if I make friends with a loser, the loser will, eventually discourage me, lower my standards, become jealous of my accomplishments, and, eventually, drag me down.

[ ] I also understand that it is possible that I can come to ruin as a consequence of my attempt to pull up an un-repentant, habitual loser. I understand that being friends with a loser can infect me with losing, as losing can be infectious and going down is easier than climbing up.

[ ] I understand that overly uncritical, overly pitiful and overly compassionate "friends" are not good for me. Their lack of criticism, too much pity and too much compassion towards me will only, gradually, lead me to mediocrity and failure.

[ ] I shall, instead, make friends with good, healthy people who will provide me with constructive criticism, worthy examples, raise my standards and save me from destructive behavior. We can mutually improve each other's lives. Iron sharpens iron.

[ ] I shall, henceforth, before I decide to help someone, first find out the cause of the person's problems. I shall not automatically assume that the person is an innocent victim of unjust life circumstances. I shall help only those that want to be helped and that can be helped.

[ ] I hereby adopt this rule of thumb: ***if I would never recommend a person to become friends with my son, father or sister, then I should never keep such a person as my friend***.

[ ] I shall not choose or keep friends that are not good for me. Neither shall I live in a place nor tolerate any conditions that are not good for me. I acknowledge that I am able and willing to change my friendships, to move, to quit or to speak out, etc. in order to improve my life.

RULE 4: COMPARE YOURSELF TO WHO YOU WERE YESTERDAY, NOT TO WHO SOMEONE ELSE IS TODAY

[ ] I acknowledge that I have an internal critic that knows all my inadequacies and failures and that always mocks my efforts to rise above mediocrity. But, the voice of this internal critic may not be wisdom. It may not be a meaningful criticism of Being.

[ ] I acknowledge that there is no equality in human ability or outcome and never will be and I am grateful for my own set of strengths and weaknesses.

[ ] I acknowledge that standards of better or worse are not illusory or unnecessary, as every activity comes with its own internal standards of accomplishment.

[ ] I shall still the voice of my internal critic by refusing to accept binary articulations of value. Instead I shall recognize a continuum of value with various degrees and gradations. Nothing is really black and white. There are millions of shades in between.

[ ] I, therefore, acknowledge that there is not just one game at which to succeed or fail in life. There are many games and some of these games match my talents.

[ ] I shall try another game, in case I do not succeed at the one I'm playing. In other words, I shall be ever ready to move, to leave, to quit, to change the game until I find something better matched to my unique mix of strengths, weaknesses and situation. In the event that changing the game does not work, I shall invent a game of my own. The point is that I should be playing only in a game that is matched to my unique mix of strengths, weaknesses and situation.

[ ] I acknowledge that I am playing many games at the same time (career, friends, family, finances, health, personal projects, and miscellaneous pursuits, etc.). I acknowledge that I will most likely perform to varying degrees of success or failure across all these games. But that is how it should be. I do not expect to win at everything!

[ ] I shall not compare myself to others in the various games I am playing. Doing so is inappropriate. I shall remain grateful for what I have, as gratitude protects me against the feelings of victimhood and resentment.

[ ] I shall work hard at becoming adventurous and truthful. I shall always articulate myself, and express what justifies my life. I shall not be afraid to express my dark and unspoken desires. I shall stop putting up with things, or pretending to like things just because of duty or obligation or because I wish to avoid conflict. I shall stop pretending to be moral.

[ ] I shall, henceforth, take stock of my flaws, faults, imperfections, inadequacies and begin to address them one at a time. I shall proceed in small steps and reward myself as I go. I shall do this for 3 years until my life is transformed.

[ ] I am willing to let go of my idiosyncratic world view, my current knowledge, so that a new world of new possibilities will show itself to me. I acknowledge that this is a vital precondition for transformative change to take place in my life.

[ ] I shall pay attention and focus on my physical and psychological environment and fix those things within my environment that bother me. To fix those things, I shall divide the task into small parts and attend to the smallest part with the least effort. With persistence and repetition, I shall eventually attain lasting change.

[ ] I shall focus on improving myself. I shall align my soul with God, with the Truth and the Good and with order and with beauty. I shall always pursue the highest good, and worry not for my sustenance or for tomorrow, because God will sustain me.

[ ] I shall always tell the truth, be ever ready to negotiate, be humble and patient. I acknowledge that I can be as good as I want to be and that no one is really better off than me and no one can be a better me than me.

[ ] I shall always ask, seek, and knock and I shall do so fervently and with conviction, as I know that I will surely be answered; that I shall surely find; and that the door shall surely be opened unto me.

[ ] Very importantly, I shall compare myself only to the me of yesterday and not to who some other person is today.

RULE 5: DO NOT LET YOUR CHILDREN DO ANYTHING THAT MAKES YOU DISLIKE THEM

[ ] I acknowledge that discipline is important for children and as a parent I shall not hesitate to discipline my children where appropriate.

[ ] I acknowledge that children are not perennially innocent thus I shall never leave my children to their own devices. Instead, I shall properly discipline, train and socialize my children so that they can become acceptable members of the society.

[ ] I acknowledge that parents are responsible for teaching children how to behave so that the children can function meaningfully within society and that this responsibility is actually an act of mercy (from parent to child) based on a long-term judgment.

[ ] I shall not (for fear of conflict, stress or resentment from my children) avoid correcting or disciplining my children.

[ ] I acknowledge as false: (a) that any form of child discipline is damaging to children; (b) that rules can only irreversibly inhibit the creativity of children; (c) that it is best to leave children alone, to their own devices, to make their own choices; (d) that there is no excuse for physical punishment (in child discipline); (e) that "hitting" a child merely teaches the child to "hit"; (f) that subjecting children to any adult's dictates (including the dictates of the child's parents) is adultism (a sort of oppression and prejudice like racism, or sexism). I repudiate and disavow all these false notions.

[ ] I acknowledge that the following tactics are available to me for the purpose of disciplining my children and that I may (using reasonable judgment) employ them or not depending on the circumstances: (a) use of reward, (b) use of threats and punishment (in appropriate proportions), (c) keeping the rules minimal and relevant, (d) use of the least

force necessary, (e) starting with the smallest possible intervention, (f) use of "timeout" to discipline kids, (g) use of physical restraint (where appropriate), (h) applying a swat on the backside to show seriousness (i) and taking more serious actions than those already mentioned (where appropriate).

[   ] I acknowledge that if parents fail to discipline and train their children properly, that the larger society will eventually mete out more severe and painful punishment to those children (for infractions and rule violations, etc.)   than the parents could have ever dished out to those children had they not shirked their duty of disciplining and properly training their children.

[   ] I acknowledge that my capacity (as a human being) to be harsh, vengeful, and wicked is real. So in disciplining my children, I must adopt an appropriate strategy that will prevent my darker and meaner side from erupting and taking over. My disciplining of my children comes and must come only from a place of overwhelming love and good will.

RULE 6: PUT YOUR HOUSE IN ORDER

[ ] I shall never permit my negative experiences (injustices, victimizations, inequities) to cause me to question the human state of Being or to curse it or to wish to destroy it.

[ ] I shall never succumb to nihilism, regardless of whatever great suffering that life may have put me through. Instead I shall keep my head up defiantly and emulate those people who despite having suffered a past of great pain, suffering and calamity, nevertheless, emerged to choose to do good, going forward, rather than evil.

[   ] I acknowledge that vengeance (even seemingly justifiable vengeance) inhibits meaningful, productive thoughts and endeavors. I shall, therefore, jettison resentment and vengefulness so that I may welcome more productive thoughts and endeavors such as working on transforming my life.

[   ] In the event that I am currently suffering, then I shall know and acknowledge that suffering is intrinsic in the human condition and that the lived experience of human life is largely tragic. But I shall never, ever dare to blame God. Or to blame nature or reality, as doing so will only end up corrupting my soul.

[   ] In the event that I am currently suffering, I shall instead, examine myself and my ways and amend my faults, as the fault is usually in the human being and not in the stars. I shall not succumb to resentment, self-defeat or self-pity and I shall not succumb to thoughts of vengeance and destruction.

[   ] But in the event that my pain, my angst, and my suffering have become so terrible and so unendurable that I have begun to lose my soul to corruption, I shall reassess my life and discard all negative elements in my life. I shall reorganize myself and put my own

house in perfect order, first, before anything. I shall cut out all my bad habits. I shall reconsider past opportunities that I had refused or ignored. I shall work harder. I shall choose peace and goodness, first and disavow conflict and evil. And I acknowledge that if I persist in taking these measures, my life, judgment, happiness, confidence, and fortunes will all eventually change for the better.

[ ] I acknowledge the importance of first calling myself to order, first putting my house in perfect order as a precondition for my world to become a better place with more ease, happiness and improvement than suffering, troubles and tragedy.

[ ] I acknowledge that tragedy, suffering, pain, calamity, stress, sorrow, etc., can all be gone from the human experience, from the human condition, if each individual decides to live right and do good. And so I have

RULE 7: PURSUE WHAT IS MEANINGFUL, NOT WHAT IS EXPEDIENT

[ ] I acknowledge that life is intertwined with pain and suffering; that pain, suffering and tragedy are the human default state of Being. But I shall never succumb to nihilism for that reason, as I equally acknowledge that sacrifice can keep pain and suffering at bay.

[ ] I shall continuously and persistently practice and become an expert at sacrificing, sharing and generosity. This is because these are bargains for a better future that will most likely cause life and fortune to be kind to me.

[   ] I acknowledge that God's favor can be gained and His wrath averted, through proper sacrifice and so I shall make a habit of sacrifice to God in order to bring me closer to God's grace and blessings.

[   ] I acknowledge that sacrifice simply means "delayed gratification"; that the greater the sacrifice, the more effective the sacrifice; and that the greatest sacrifice is of self and/or child.

[   ] I shall emulate Socrates in that I shall not lie. Instead I shall stand by the truth regardless of the circumstances. I shall always be guided by my conscience and I shall adhere to the highest ideals. I shall live properly and I shall do the Good, for the rest of my life.

[   ] I shall do my best to reduce or eliminate unnecessary and pointless pain, suffering and misery in the lives of specific individuals and in this world. Doing so is an axiomatic good.

[   ] I acknowledge that for me to advance my state of Being, I must abandon expediency, gratuitous pleasure, and selfishness and seek only the attainment of ultimate meaning, the Good, only.

[   ] I shall not pursue expedience and selfish immediate gratification. Expedience is irresponsibility. It is superficial, faithless, lacks courage, and it is wrong. Expedience is thoughtless, instant, impulsive unrestrained and parochial and its products are only momentary and short-lived. Worst of all, expedience contains no sacrifice! So I shall shun expedience. Instead I shall aspire for and seek only that which is meaningful.

RULE 8: TELL THE TRUTH

[   ] I acknowledge that telling some truths can be harsh and unpalatable and may cause discomfort to me and or my audience. But, nevertheless, I shall tell the truth regardless of the circumstances or consequences?

[   ] I acknowledge that even the so-called white lies (however well-meant) can produce unintended consequences. Lies distort the substance of Being. They corrupt both the soul and the society alike. Therefore, I shall not tell lies (even the so-called white lies).

[   ] I acknowledge that using language, words, actions or perceptions to manipulate the world into delivering to me, my own false or misrepresented version of reality is the same as lying. Spinning reality is also the same as lying and lying does not improve reality, so I shall not engage in such an act. I shall not lie.

[   ] I shall tell the truth at all times. Even when I find myself in a situation where I don't know what to do or say, I shall simply tell the truth.

[   ] I shall not base my life on deceit and misrepresentation or "acting politically" or spinning reality. Living in this manner is living a life-lie and living a life-lie weakens character and the ability to withstand adversity.

[   ] I shall neither avoid confrontation/conflict, nor hide in a niche, nor in the routine, nor in the familiar. Living in such a manner is also living a type of life-lie that robs the individual of vitality and suppresses potentials, yet does not offer any protection from suffering.

[   ] I shall reveal myself to others, instead of avoiding and hiding. Doing so will give me access to new information with which to rebuild and renew myself.

[   ] Most importantly, I shall always reveal myself to myself. I shall never hide myself from myself.

[ ] I acknowledge that the truth will preserve my soul and protect me against the vagaries, tribulations and tragedies of life. It will also protect me from myself. I shall, therefore, always tell the truth to others and, very importantly, to myself.

RULE 9: ASSUME THAT THE PERSON YOU ARE LISTENING TO MIGHT KNOW SOMETHING YOU DON'T

[ ] I acknowledge that true thinking can be very difficult but that through talking, I can facilitate my thinking.

[ ] I acknowledge that I need to improve my listening skills; that I can learn a lot from people, from their experiences and their mistakes (just by listening to them attentively); that indeed, every conversation is a special and valuable opportunity for me to learn something new; so that listening to people can help me to improve my life. Therefore, I shall henceforth listen attentively to anyone with whom I am engaged in conversation.

[ ] I respect the honor, value and opportunity in a conversation, therefore, I shall not pervert a conversation into a struggle for power and dominance or into a monologue dominated by me or become inattentive to the conversation.

[ ] I shall henceforth make a habit of summarizing the speech/message of the party with whom I am engaged in conversation, as I acknowledge that doing so facilitates the way for a good conversation.

[ ] I shall henceforth also make a habit of listening to myself so as to be in tune and in peace with my Being.

[ ] I shall henceforth assume that the person I am listening to has some rare nuggets of information, truth, wisdom and opportunity to deliver to me.

[ ] Indeed, I acknowledge that, generally, people will tell one everything in their heads, if only one can listen attentively and patiently.

[ ] I also acknowledge that good listening/ good conversation can transform people because it is an opportunity and a platform for the mutual exchange of respect, goodwill, truth, wisdom and empowering information and opportunities.

[ ] So, again, I shall henceforth listen attentively, patiently and respectfully to whoever I am conversing with.

RULE 10: BE PRECISE WITH YOUR SPEECH

[   ] I acknowledge that precision simplifies things and that precision brings order, definition, clarity and habitability to my world.

[   ] I shall henceforth, therefore be precise and not leave things vague.

[   ] I shall henceforth mind what I tell myself and others and I shall use only appropriate and precise words in speaking to myself and to others.

[   ] I shall henceforth not hide from, avoid or tolerate imprecision in my life. I shall engage with it and correct it whenever it materializes in my life. I shall never ignore it.

[   ] I shall henceforth be precise in my conversations (even the difficult conversations). This means that I shall define or acknowledge the topic of each conversation and stick to that topic without deviating.

[   ] I shall henceforth be precise in my plans, objectives, goals and ambition, as doing so makes it more likely that I may achieve them.

[   ] I shall henceforth be precise in my words and deeds because precision in speech and actions is a pathway through which I can discover meaning in my life and protect myself from tragedy.

RULE 11: LEAVE CHILDREN ALONE WHEN THEY ARE SKATEBOARDING

[   ] I acknowledge that overprotection robs children of the opportunity of developing important life skills that would enable them to face danger and defeat fear and doubt later on in their lives. Overprotection prepares children for failure when faced with serious challenges in the future.

[   ] I shall henceforth, therefore not overprotect my children.

[   ] Because I agree with Peterson, I shall raise my boys to become men.
OR
[   ] Because I disagree with Peterson, I shall raise my boys without inculcating any gender stereotypes in them. (*Cancel whichever does not apply*)

[   ] I shall not disturb children when they are skate-boarding (or engaging in some brave but minimally "dangerous" physical activity). I acknowledge that they'll tumble and fall and scrape, but then, they would have also engaged, learnt, toughened up and prepared themselves to be able to face and overcome danger and serious challenges in the future. And that is a good thing.

RULE 12: PET A CAT WHEN YOU ENCOUNTER ONE ON THE STREET

[   ] I acknowledge that life is suffering; that human beings are intrinsically fragile, breakable, vulnerable, and destructible; that limitations, vulnerability and fragility are the immutable conditions of Being; that these are what make us human; and that this is the human reality, the human condition, the human state of Being.

[   ] I shall not succumb to despair, despondency or hatred and contemplate the destruction of Being or curse Being (despite the pain, suffering, limitations and vulnerabilities of Being). Instead I shall employ truth, precision, responsibility, accountability, sacrifice, meaning and M&Ms to keep the limitations of Being at bay.

[   ] I acknowledge that being human implies imperfection, limitation, vulnerability fragility, etc. But I also acknowledge that the existence of limitation and vulnerability in one human triggers love for that human from another human. So, it may not be entirely bad to be limited and vulnerable. I accept my vulnerabilities. Perfection is not being human.

[   ] This is a wonderful life, a beautiful life (despite its many thorns)! I shall make sure that I enjoy my life and the many M&Ms that come with it! I shall celebrate the wonder of Being. So, I shall enjoy life's little pleasures from this day forward!!!

NOTES

Printed by Amazon Italia Logistica S.r.l.
Torrazza Piemonte (TO), Italy

13073975R00066